Contents

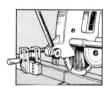

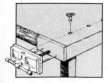
From your friends at
Better Homes and Gardens®

Dear Fellow Woodworker,
In *WOOD*® magazine, the column TIPS FROM YOUR SHOP (AND OURS) has consistently ranked as the best-read feature we publish. It seems that our readers just can't get enough of these helpful workshop hints. And I think I know why. In woodworking, no one knows it all. But through experience, we all run onto better, faster, safer, or easier ways to do things in our shop. And it's these little nuggets of wisdom that over time make us all better at working with wood.

We're always hearing from readers who want us to publish a collection of the best shop tips that have appeared in *WOOD* magazine. Well, here they are, all 335 of them, hot off the press. We've organized the tips, all of which appeared in issues 1 through 35, into 24 short chapters so you can locate them easily. And we've included an index on page 96, also for your convenience. Here's hoping that you find many ideas in this publication that you can put to good use in your shop.

Happy woodworking,

Larry Clayton

Larry Clayton
Editor, *WOOD* Magazine

335 GREAT SHOP TIPS
Editor: Larry Clayton
Managing Editor: Bill Krier
Designer: Mike Harrington
Cover Illustration: Mark Marturello
©COPYRIGHT Meredith Corporation, 1991.
All Rights Reserved.
Printed in the U.S.A.

Bandsaw Helpers

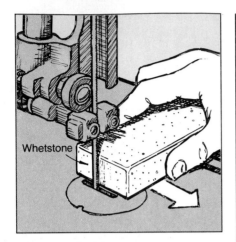

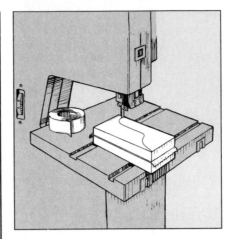

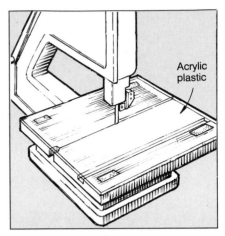

Acrylic plastic

Glass-smooth cuts

Generally, bandsaw blades make pretty rough cuts. How can you get smoother cuts?

TIP: This trick works best on ⅛" fine-tooth blades, when cutting stock ¾" thick or less. To get a super-smooth cut use a coarse whetstone to hone the sides of the blade as shown in the drawing *above*. This removes the "set" on the teeth.

Note: After doing this, the blade will cut slower and hotter.

—From the *WOOD* magazine shop

Quick 'n' easy bandsaw extension table

Sometimes you may find your bandsaw table too skimpy to support the work. And you don't want to spend time making a complicated table extension.

TIP: Cut a piece of ¾" plywood to the size needed, then cut out a slot to admit the bandsaw blade, as shown at *right*. Clamp the plywood extension to the table. If you want to rip wide stock, clamp or screw a wood fence to the table extension, parallel with the bandsaw blade. Support long boards with a stand positioned on the outfeed side of the saw.

—Don Butler, Waterford, Pa.

Pairing project pieces

Cutting exact duplicates can be difficult. If you use nails to join the pieces, there are holes to fill. With staples, it's necessary to restaple the parts as wood is sawed away.

TIP: Carbon copies won't slip apart when sawing if you use double-faced carpet tape to join them. Make your layout off the top piece of stock, then apply the tape to its back side. Remove the protective strip from the tape and firmly press the pieces together in alignment. Don't worry about tape placement between the blocks, as the saw blade won't be hindered.

—From the *WOOD* magazine shop

Slick solution for ribbed bandsaw tables

The grooves tooled into the table surface of some bandsaws can interfere with the movement of small wood pieces while you're sawing them.

TIP: Attaching an overlay sheet of ¼" clear acrylic plastic to the top of the table provides a slick work surface for cutting small pieces. Saw a kerf halfway into the acrylic sheet so it's aligned with all four table edges, as shown *above*. Cut or notch an opening for the table-leveling screw, if necessary. Tape the sheet to the tabletop with small strips of double-faced tape.

—Bob Ward, Lakewood, Ohio

Whetstone

Blemish Cover-ups

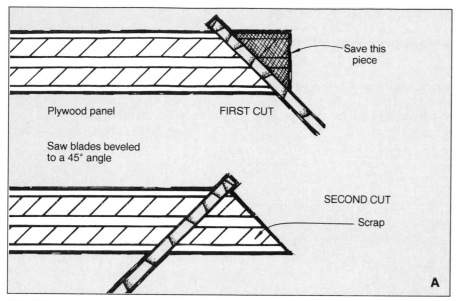

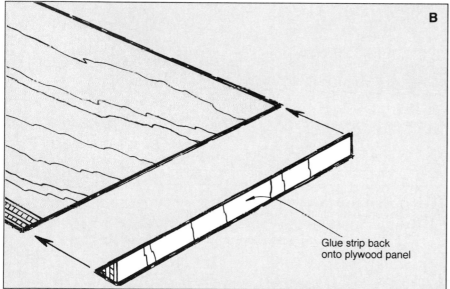

Save this piece

Plywood panel   FIRST CUT

Saw blades beveled
to a 45° angle

SECOND CUT

Scrap

A

B

Glue strip back
onto plywood panel

Hide edges in plywood and other materials

Panels constructed of hardwood-faced plywood have pretty faces, but the laminated edges simply are not presentable on cabinetry or other projects. Veneering is a possible solution—providing you have the materials and tools to do the job.

TIP: To disguise the plywood layers, cut beveled strips from the material with your tablesaw or radial-arm saw set at 45° as shown in Drawing A. Make a second cut perpendicular to the first one as shown and discard the resulting scrap. Finally, glue the first strip in place as shown in Drawing B. This procedure also extends the face-grain pattern onto the edge. You can also use this technique to disguise freshly sawed edges on weathered barn boards used for picture frames.

—Howard Pieplow, West Allis, Wis.

Smooth repairs are a matter of a close shave

The success of making inconspicuous finish repairs depends on achieving as smooth a surface as possible with a putty stick of the correct color.

TIP: Make sure the touch-up material is about body temperature so it lays on an adequate layer easily. For a really smooth surface, remove the excess putty with a disposable razor blade as shown *below.*

—Paul C. Krueger III, Wharton, N.J.

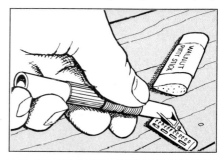

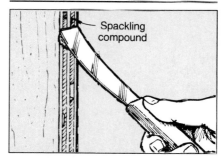

Spackling compound

Surprise filler for plywood edges

How do you get the exposed edges of plywood smooth enough so they look like solid wood when painted? Using wood putty as a filler and sanding will do the job, but there's got to be an easier way.

TIP: Use exterior spackling compound to fill plywood edges. It's easier to sand than wood putty, dries quickly, and is less expensive, too. Sand smooth with 60- and 120-grit sandpaper.

—Janet H. Sparks, Lexington, Ky.

Blemish Cover-ups

Perfect plywood patch

You need a small piece of AA or AB plywood and all you have in the shop is CD with a knothole.

TIP: Cut a scrap piece of plywood, ⅛" veneer, or resawn solid stock the thickness of the depression to an inch or so longer and wider than the knothole. Lay a piece of carbon paper, carbon side up, over the hole and place the patching piece over it (make sure the wood grain runs in the same direction). Rap the top piece with a hammer to imprint the knothole onto the scrap.

Cut out the shape, spread glue in the knothole, and press the patch into place. Sand flush.

—Russell E. Price, Barneveld, N.Y.

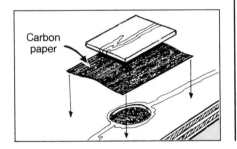

Carbon paper

Stir up a super wood filler

Because wood putty never seems to exactly match the wood, patches stick out like a sore thumb.

TIP: For an exact color match, there's nothing closer than the actual wood. Gather fresh sawdust—the finer the better—from your belt sander or workbench. On waxed paper, stir epoxy cement with the sawdust. Fill holes, cracks, and mistakes with the mixture.

—From the *WOOD* magazine shop

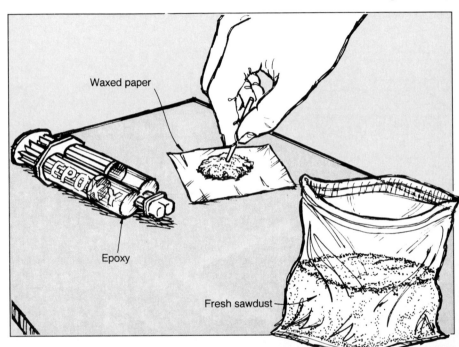

Waxed paper

Epoxy

Fresh sawdust

Raising dents and scratches

Even the smallest dents and scratches mar the appearance of otherwise successful woodworking projects.

TIP: To remove small dents or raise minor scratches in wood surfaces, wet and then cover the problem area with a damp cloth. Using a household iron on a dry setting, apply heat to the cloth for 15-second intervals. Take care not to scorch the wood.

—From the *WOOD* magazine shop

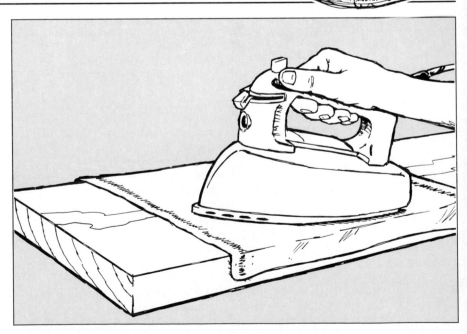

Miter clamp blocks

Sometimes, clamp blocks become glued to the miter joint.

TIP: Cut practically glue-proof ones from blocks of scrap plywood or hardwood. Make your cuts in the order shown here. The fourth cut is a chamfer that provides space between the block and the joint so squeeze-out won't adhere.

—From the *WOOD* magazine shop

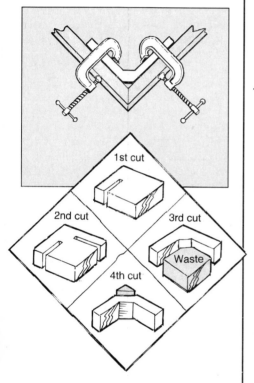

1st cut

2nd cut

3rd cut

Waste

4th cut

Spring miter clamps

All of a sudden you can't find the miter clamps. Misplaced? Lost? In use? What to do?

TIP: Make extras you'll always have around from an old coil spring about the size found in a mattress. Clip out a section with cutters, then twist or bend until it lies flat. File each end of the piece to a point (the sharper the point, the better it will hold). After gluing the joint, spread the clamp with both hands and place on the joint as shown at *right*. Later, fill and sand the holes left by the springs.

—From the *WOOD* magazine shop

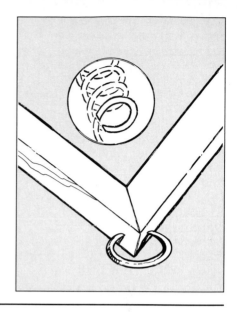

Oh, go soak your wood!

Bending laminations into tight curves can be mighty tricky work. The laminations may pop apart after gluing and irregular grain may split.

TIP: The night before you plan to laminate, run hot tap water over the pieces or soak them in a tub of hot water for a few minutes. Then, place the pieces in the form and clamp overnight. This preforming, though not a cure-all by any means, reduces some of the tendency for laminates to separate and for irregular grain to split.

—Cliff Miller, Loretta, Wis.

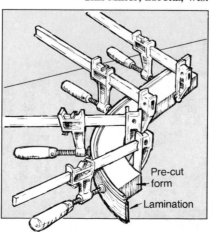

Pre-cut form

Lamination

Shims that don't fall off your pipe clamps

When banding plywood or edge-joining stock, it helps to use thin scraps of wood as shims or spacers to raise the workpiece above the clamp's pipe. Unfortunately, these scraps fall out and are a pain to manage while you're setting up your clamps.

TIP: For ¾" pipe clamps, cut 1" lengths of 1" PVC pipe. Make one longitudinal cut in each one so it slides easily along the pipe and slips on as shown in the drawing *below*. For ½" pipe clamps, cut the shims from ¾" PVC pipe. These split rings elevate the work about ⅛" from the pipe, putting it closer to the center of the jaws.

—Terry L. Davis, Ft. Pierce, Fla.

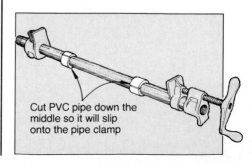

Cut PVC pipe down the middle so it will slip onto the pipe clamp

Clamping

Inexpensive frame clamps from cabinet hinges

Relatively high cost keeps some woodworkers from appreciating the convenience of commercially available picture-frame clamps.

TIP: Make this picture-frame clamp with four 4″ strap hinges, four 18″ lengths of 5/16″ threaded rod, and 12 nuts. First, at the ends of the hinges, ream holes large enough to accept the threaded rods, and then bend right angles into the leaves. For assembling smaller picture frames, you may wish to cut a set of shorter threaded rods.

—George A. Heffelfinger, Lehighton, Pa.

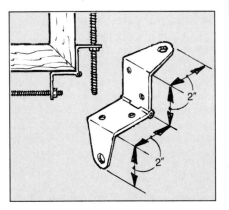

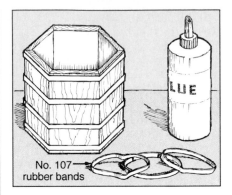

The original "band" clamp

Although it's fairly routine to glue flat surfaces, you find it difficult to get even pressure on round, irregular, or otherwise out-of-the-ordinary surfaces.

TIP: For less than $2 at most office supply stores, you can purchase an ordinary ½-lb. box of no. 107 rubber bands. The bands, which measure 1/16″ thick, 5/8″ wide, and 7″ long before stretching, make great clamps. Smaller bands also can be useful in the shop. The glue pops off easily, and they never rust. (By the way, the bands will last a lot longer if you store them in a cool, dark drawer.)

—Mike Locke, Long Beach, Calif.

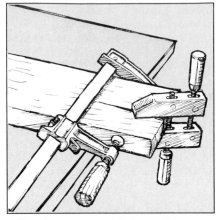

Aligning a rough break

When gluing split or broken pieces back together, how do you keep the break or split perfectly aligned during the gluing and clamping process?

TIP: First remove any loose splinters that will interfere with the fit. With a flat stick, spatula, or feeler-gauge blade, work the glue into the break. Then use a handscrew, or a combination of blocks and clamps, to align the adjacent faces, as shown in the drawing *above*. Finally, position another clamp at right angles to the break to pull it together.

—Don Butler, Waterford, Pa.

Magnets keep your clamp pads in place

When using clamps, it's a good idea to sandwich wood spacers between the jaws and project to keep from marring it. But how do you keep the scrap in position while tightening the clamp?

TIP: Recess small, round hobby magnets into 2″ squares of ½″ plywood. Drill the recess holes just deep enough so the magnet projects slightly above the face of the block, then epoxy the magnet in place. The magnets hold the blocks on the clamp jaws while you're clamping.

—William M. Resnik, Albuquerque, N.M.

Clamping

Stay-in-place clamp pads

When clamping glued-up stock, the pads you use between the clamp jaws and the stock fall out before you can even tighten the clamps.

TIP: Add top flanges to your pads as shown to form L-shaped devices that ride on top of as well as against the material you're clamping. Make several, using hardboard or thin plywood glued and screwed to your normal pad material. Keep them handy for the times you use pipe or bar clamps.

—From the *WOOD* magazine shop

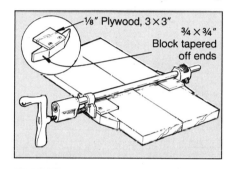

⅛" Plywood, 3×3"

¾ × ¾" Block tapered off ends

Do the clamping two-step

Unless you have help, struggling with pipe clamps to clamp a mitered box or frame for gluing can be tough.

TIP: Call a strap clamp to the rescue. Glue and assemble the project at the workbench. First secure the workpieces with a strap clamp and then beef up the clamping process with pipe clamps, as shown *above*.

—From the *WOOD* magazine shop

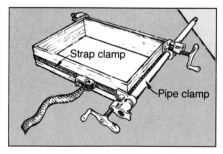

Strap clamp

Pipe clamp

Can't hold it all up? Look, Ma, more hands!

Make a clamping error and you'll pay in time and sweat. Sometimes it seems as if a person needs three or four hands to tighten pipe or bar clamps without allowing the boards to slip. This is especially true when you try to insert wood scraps to prevent the clamps from marring the project material.

TIP: Cut clamping blocks out of scrap wood or plywood the appropriate size in a suitable shape to fit the clamp (see illustration *below*) and drive tacks or small nails into the edges. Loop rubber bands over the clamp jaws to hold the blocks in place before tightening.

—Dave Tobey, Fort Worth, Texas

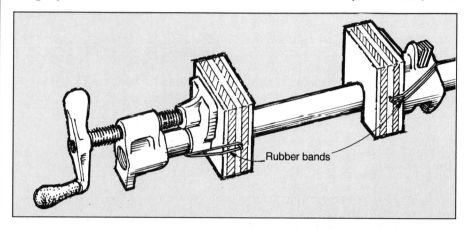

Rubber bands

Pressed for a good clamp?

Sometimes you just don't have the right size clamp for clamping odd-shaped projects such as ring bowls and vases.

TIP: Use your drill press. Center the workpiece on your drill-press table. Apply pressure with the quill, using a scrap piece of wood in between to protect the project. Then lock the quill in position. This works well on projects where ordinary clamps aren't deep enough to fit.

—F.F. Kuhn, Cedarcreek, Mo.

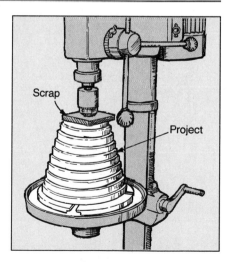

Scrap

Project

Clamping

Great holding device for odd situations

Toolmakers have been truly ingenious in designing a wide variety of clamps and hold-downs for woodworkers. Even so, puzzling situations arise when nothing fits an irregular-shaped workpiece, such as a carving.

TIP: A strap clamp that uses a pressure pedal to hold workpieces on a bench often solves these off-the-wall quandaries. Materials needed include 4' of 1"-wide canvas strap, a panhead screw and washer to attach one end of the strap to the bottom of the workbench, a 1' length of 2×4 to serve as a pressure pedal, and pieces of hook-and-loop fastener to adjust the length of the strap. Cut slots in the bench top and assemble the pieces as shown. This arrangement will hold workpieces of most any shape and allows you to quickly reposition the workpiece.

—**Jerry Rakoezy, Rawlins, Wyo.**

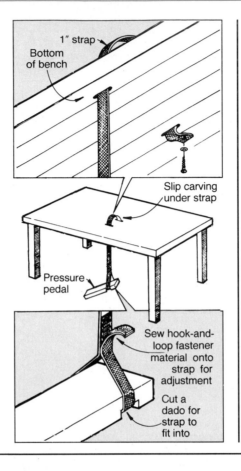

1" strap
Bottom of bench
Slip carving under strap
Pressure pedal
Sew hook-and-loop fastener material onto strap for adjustment
Cut a dado for strap to fit into

New angle on gluing corners

Triangular blocks often slip when clamping mitered corners.

TIP: Double-faced carpet tape to the rescue again! A layer of tape on one surface of a triangular block makes a world of difference when clamping mitered corners. After the glue has dried, save the blocks and reuse them on your next project. (Stay away from thin double-faced tapes that don't have a lot of sticking power.)

—**Marvin C. Betcher, Davenport, Iowa**

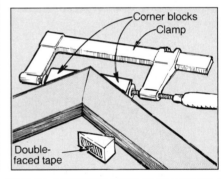

Corner blocks
Clamp
Double-faced tape

Picture this: better cabinets

One person can struggle trying to assemble a box or cabinet.

TIP: No matter what type of joints you've cut, a picture-frame clamp works like another pair of hands in the workshop. Position two adjoining sides and tighten a corner clamp over the joint. Repeat the procedure with an adjoining joint. Now loosen a clamp, reposition the pieces to an accurate fit and tighten. Join the pieces with screws or nails and repeat the procedure with the other joints.

—**David W. Schweizer, Fellsmere, Fla.**

Woodworker's clamps glue edges, too

You can't top edge clamps for edge-gluing projects, but like all quality tools, a fistful of them represents a tidy investment. Without denting your wallet, wouldn't it be nice if clamps you already own would work for this task?

TIP: Call your woodworker's clamps into action for those occasional edge-gluing jobs by using them in combination with homemade wooden wedges. After fitting together the glued workpieces, tighten the clamps in place as shown at *right* and tap wedges in place for the desired lateral pressure. Suitably sized C-clamps work quite well in this arrangement, too.

—**From the *WOOD* magazine shop**

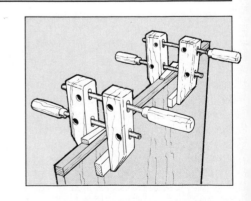

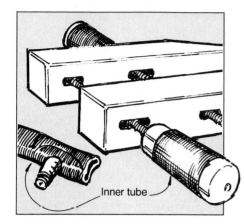

Get a grip on handscrews

You can apply considerable pressure with handscrews, but some of us have difficulty gripping the smooth handles.

TIP: Old bicycle inner tubes provide an inexpensive, quick solution to this gripping problem. Use baby or talcum powder to help stretch and position the inner tube on the handles as shown at *left.*

—Calvin W. Henne, Bridgeport, Neb.

Mini frame clamps

You're gluing up a picture frame and don't have a frame clamp small enough to hold it.

TIP: Make a miniature frame clamp like the one shown in the drawing *below.* You'll need four small inside corner braces, four rubber bands, and eight ¾" flathead machine screws with nuts and washers. Attach the screws to the braces as shown, to hold the rubber bands. Simply position the braces at the frame corners and stretch the rubber bands between them to hold the frame pieces in place.

—Joe Baltz, Joliet, Ill.

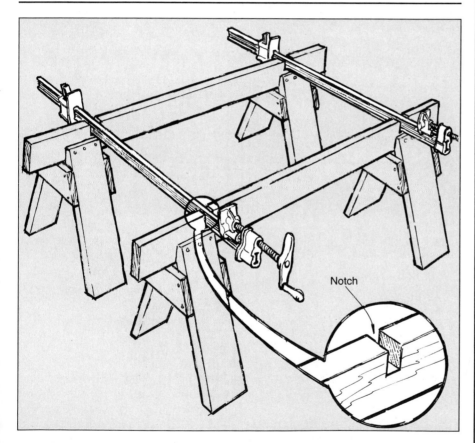

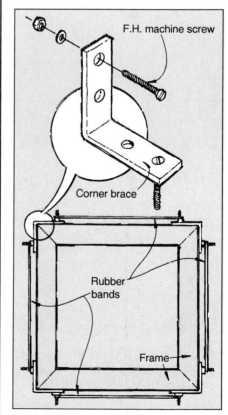

Horsing around with bar clamps

Many woodworkers don't have a large enough clamping table for doors and other wide objects. And, bar clamps have a tendency to flop to one side when laid on a flat surface.

TIP: Summon a couple of sawhorses to the rescue. Notch the horses and insert your bar clamps or pipe clamps, as shown in the drawing *above.* For flat sawhorses and workbenches, notch two 2×4s in a similar fashion and tack them to the work surface.

—Rob Huffman, Danville, Va.

Dealing with Dust

These connectors keep sawdust out of motors

Fine sawdust can turn up in surprising places—such as inside totally enclosed motors and electrical boxes on table and radial-arm saws, drill presses, and the like. This invasion, which can shorten motor life and pose a fire hazard, may result from power cords being held with Romex connectors that permit the infiltration of fine dust.

TIP: Replace Romex connectors with flexible cord and power-cable connectors. Their liquid-tight connectors successfully block the dust invasion. You'll find them in all knockout sizes and a wide range of cable sizes. If your hardware store doesn't have them, an electrical-supply dealer should.

—C. Clay Milner, Atlanta

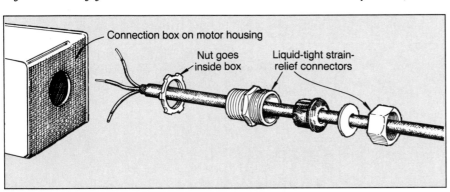

Connection box on motor housing

Nut goes inside box

Liquid-tight strain-relief connectors

Workshop dust trap

Many power tool jobs produce a haze of powdery sawdust that drifts and settles everywhere. It's particularly irritating in your basement or garage.

TIP: Build a dust collector from a large cardboard box (or use plywood), then fit it with replaceable furnace filters on three or four sides and a room fan that expels filtered air from one side.

—David L. Wiseley, Waters, Mich.

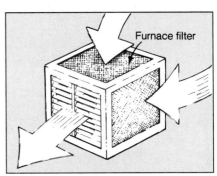

Furnace filter

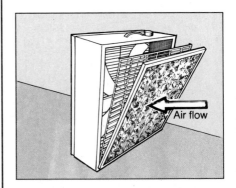

Air flow

When dust gets in your eyes

You can get lost in a cloud of dust when working with an orbital or belt sander. The dust obscures your work, to say nothing of restricting comfortable breathing.

TIP: Blow those troubles away with a small, nonoscillating household fan placed 3 or 4 feet away from the sander you're using. The trick is to turn the fan to a low speed and place it at a right angle to your work and to remove the dust without raising a dust storm. In small shops, however, this may cause an airborne dust problem.

—From the *WOOD* magazine shop

Simplified dust collector

Sawing and sanding operations generate a lot of irritating fine dust in the workshop.

TIP: Here's a simpler alternative to the shop tip at *top*. Install a furnace filter on one side of a box with wire or bungee cord. Position the fan adjacent to the work area so it pulls air away from you. Clean the filters periodically with a shop vacuum.

—James R. Loshinsky, Youngstown, Ohio

Quick, clean drilling guide

It's a challenge to center the holes on the opposite side of a butt or dado joint for a divider or shelf. You can mark the line with a faint pencil, but you'll do extra sanding on the unfinished wood to remove each mark, no matter how faint.

TIP: Place a strip of masking tape matching the width of the divider or shelf along the desired line, mark the hole locations on it, then drill away. The tape reduces the chances of chipping, and it pulls off easily without leaving layout marks.

—Don Oliver, Nederland, Texas

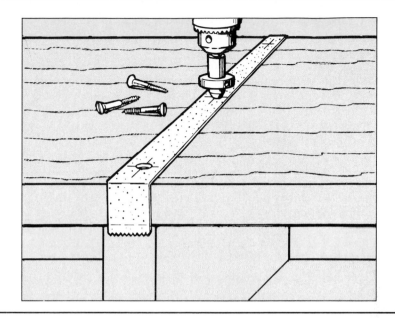

Here's how to center a bit in an existing hole

Enlarging a hole in wood or other material requires a lot of guesswork to start the bit in the exact center.

TIP: Insert a scrap of dowel the diameter of the existing hole and slightly recessed from the surface—about ¹⁄₁₆″. Fit a drill bit the same size as the hole into the recess and tap the end of the shank just hard enough to mark the dowel center. Use this mark to start drilling the larger hole.

—Ed Good, Nordland, Wash.

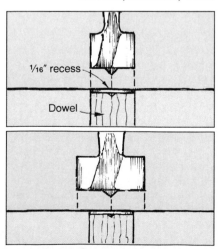

¹⁄₁₆″ recess

Dowel

Round stock drill guide

Drilling a lot of holes in line with one another and perpendicular to the same plane can be a real challenge in round stock.

TIP: Cut a scrap wood block large enough to level with the bottom of the V-shaped notches on your drill-guide base. Then place one end of the round stock into the guide and place the block under it. Drill through the stock and into the block. Now move the pieces out from under the drill guide and pin them together with a short dowel. As shown in the drawing *above,* you'll now be able to drill as many holes as you need, where you want them, by simply positioning the block the appropriate distance away from the drill each time.

—From the *WOOD* magazine shop

Drilling

Sacking a mess before it becomes one

Drilling holes in wall paneling, especially drywall, leaves unsightly particles on the wall and the floor, fine dusty material that's tough to clean up.

TIP: Tape an open paper bag to the wall a few inches below where you plan to drill. Once that bit starts chewing and spitting out nasty particles, they fall right into the sack. When finished drilling, simply pull loose the masking tape, and toss away a mess that never happened.

—**Earl Hagen, Livonia, Mich.**

Jaws III

There's a good reason three-jawed Jacobs chucks used on portable electric drills, drill presses, and most lathes have three evenly spaced holes for inserting the chuck key.

TIP: When tightening the chuck, use the key in all three holes—not just one. This applies equally distributed pressure on the jaws, so bit and accessory shanks won't slip.

—**John Seminew, Crete, Ill.**

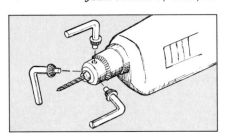

Bull's-eye alignment for large-diameter holes

Centering a Forstner bit on a workpiece can be difficult because the shape of the cutting head prevents you from seeing its point and your layout lines.

TIP: Drill a 1/16" guide hole at the centerpoint of each hole. Ease the tip of the bit into the guide hole and take care to keep it in place as you turn on the drill press.

—**From the *WOOD* magazine shop**

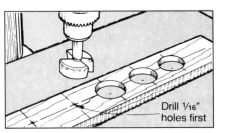

Drill 1/16" holes first

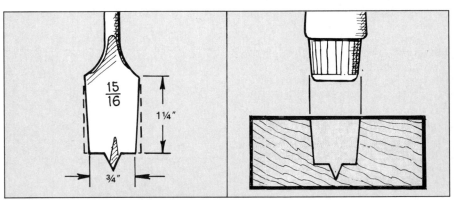

Taper a bit to fit plugs and candles

It's sometimes hard to get wood plugs to fit snugly into the holes you've drilled for them, especially if you're working with softwoods. Also, when boring holes for conventional taper candles 8" to 12" long, a standard spade bit will not produce a snug fit. The holes will be either too large at the bottom, which permits the candle to flop back and forth, or too small for the base to be inserted properly.

TIP: Grind a *slight* taper on the cutting edges of some spade bits. With these tapered bits, plugs will fit into their holes like a cork into a bottle. Just a few strokes of the file or a pass or two over the grinder will suffice. Make sure both sides of the bit have identical tapers.

For candles, modify a spade bit of the appropriate size—15/16" matches standard tapered candles. Scribe lines on the bit so it tapers from a 15/16" diameter to 3/4" as shown *above*.

—**John Wolf, St. Joseph, Mich.**

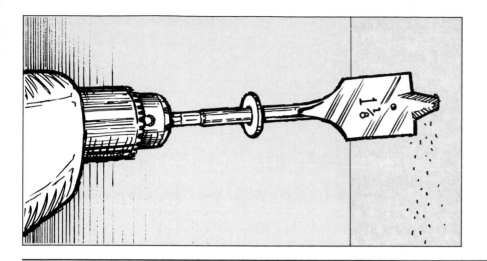

On-the-level procedure for drilling perpendicular holes

When using a hand-held electric drill, it's nearly impossible to determine if your bit is perpendicular to the surface.

TIP: Here's an easy aid if you're drilling parallel to the floor with spade bits. Before inserting the bit into the chuck, slip a large washer over the shaft. If the bit is parallel to the floor, the washer will neither climb up nor walk down the shank.

—Robert A. Grace, St. Joseph, Mich.

Drill-bit straightener

Small-diameter drill bits are easily bent during normal use.

TIP: To straighten a bent bit, chuck it into your drill and, while running the drill at full speed, insert the drill point into a piece of scrap wood. Apply slight sideways pressure to the drill to return the bit to its proper shape. When you release the pressure, the bit will continue to run true.

—Robert S. Tupper, Canton, S.D.

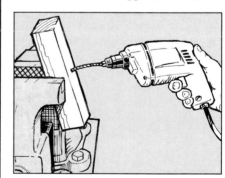

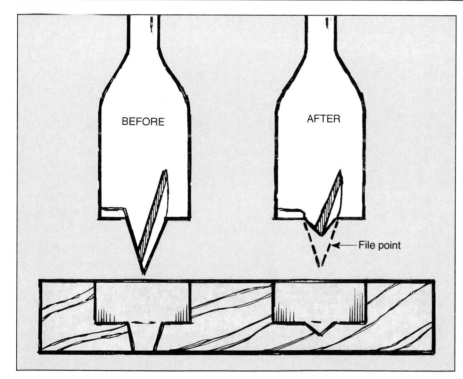

BEFORE

AFTER

← File point

File away a boring problem

Without using an expensive Forstner bit, it's next to impossible to bore holes without breaking through the opposite side (e.g., when drilling a ½"-deep hole in ¾" stock).

TIP: By filing down the point of a spade bit you can achieve the depth of cut you want without breaking through the other side. Even if you buy an extra spade bit just for this use, it still is cheaper than a Forstner bit.

—Charles Hughes, Hamburg, N.Y.

Drilling

Depth-of-hole control

Without a drill press, accurate control of hole depth with an electric drill is difficult at best.

TIP: Drill a hole in a short length of dowel that's large enough in diameter that it won't split and fits snugly on the bit. To adjust for depth of the hole, vary the dowel's length and the placement of the bit in the chuck. You can make several of these for a variety of depths and bit sizes to keep on hand, or toss it when finished.

—From the *WOOD* magazine shop

Catch-all for overhead drilling

Afraid to look up when drilling overhead with your portable electric drill because you get an eyeful of shavings? Try this solution next time.

TIP: Slip a plastic-foam or paper cup (cut down to size for short bits) over the drill bit. Pull it back against the chuck so you can see to start the hole. Then push it up and finish drilling the hole. The cup should catch all of the debris.

—Robert G. Fleischman, Verona, Pa.

Nonsmashing success

Ouch! Some drill presses have nothing to prevent the table from crashing to the floor. If this has happened to you, it will likely happen again. Will your toes be in the path next time?

TIP: Prevent the next accident from happening. An inexpensive 3″ muffler clamp fits around most drill-press columns. Clamp it as a safety support about 2″ above the base so you can handle large projects without worrying about your toes.

—John Sokolovich, New Oxford, Pa.

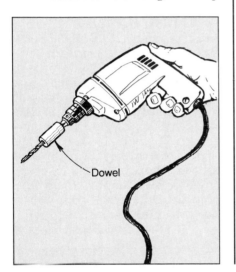

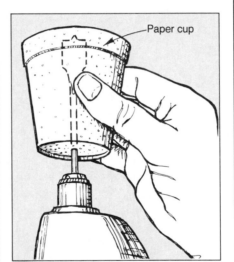

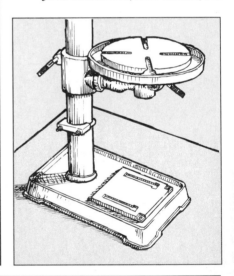

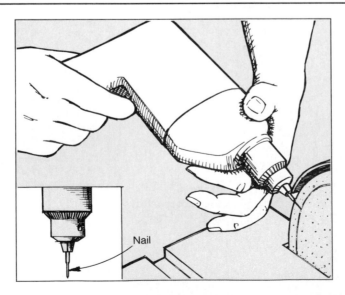

Filling the need for a tiny bit

Every once in a while, you find yourself lacking the precise size of drill bit to do a particular job. This happens especially often in small diameters.

TIP: Use a small finishing nail or brad in place of a standard bit. Snip or hacksaw off the head before putting it into the drill chuck. With the nail held securely in the chuck, grind the nail down by rotating it as you hold the side of the nail against a grinding stone or sanding disc as shown at *left*.

—From the *WOOD* magazine shop

Fastening and Gluing

Rescue a hinge
It's easy for a project to come unhinged when screws break off.

TIP: Don't drive a new screw at a different angle or even consider moving the hinge. Instead, drill and countersink a new hole next to the troublesome hole in the hinge. Drill a pilot hole and wax or soap the new screw before driving it. Snip off a shortened, properly sized screw and drive it into the defective hole to cover up.

—William Cox, Rolling Meadows, Ill.

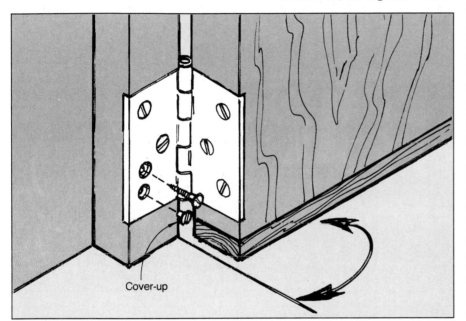
Cover-up

Blot up squeezed-out glue
Some glue squeeze-out is normal when clamping joints, but letting it dry makes it tough to remove later.

TIP: Sprinkle coarse sawdust along the joint to blot up the freshly squeezed-out, wet glue, then scrape or wipe it up immediately. Follow with a handful of fine sawdust rubbed into and over the area to pick up any remaining glue particles.

—Paul Branton, Mt. Olive, Miss.

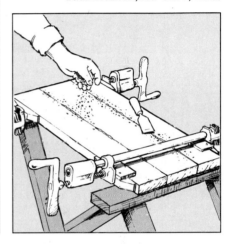

Rx for filling tiny cavities
Getting glue into tiny hairline cracks can be tough. Sometimes, even a toothpick may not do the trick without considerable mess.

TIP: At your next dental check-up, ask your dentist if he'll part with some of his worn dental probes—the type with a tough, thread-size wire attached to each end of the handle. With them, you can easily and accurately spread glue into extremely narrow cracks.

—L.E. Spotts, Slater, Mo.

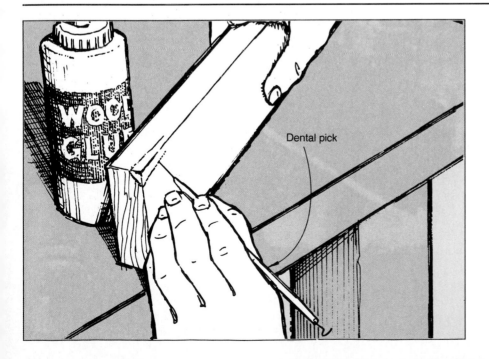
Dental pick

Fastening and Gluing

Drat! Another broken screw

Many a woodworker has uttered a foul word after accidentally twisting off the head of a wood screw while driving it into dense wood. And more such words usually follow while trying to undo the mess.

TIP: Here's a four-step process for removing the broken screw and repairing the damage:

1 Equip your drill with a 3/32" twist bit, then drill holes all the way around the screw, slightly deeper than its length.

2 Back out the screw with a pair of needle-nose pliers.

3 Drill out the damaged area, using a 5/16" or 3/8" bit, and glue in a suitable length of hardwood dowel of the proper width.

4 Using the correct-size screw pilot bit, drill a pilot hole into the dowel for the new screw.

After you insert the screw the area should look nearly normal.

—Bruce Vandermark, Syracuse, Ind.

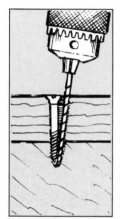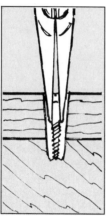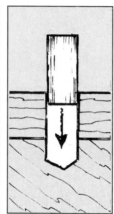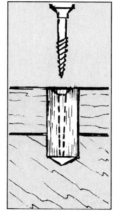

Avoiding nail splits

Even though you hammer carefully, your nail occasionally splits the wood.

TIP: Blunt the tip of the nail by tapping it with your hammer to let the nail hit its way into the wood rather than part the material. Or, chuck a properly sized nail into a drill (you may need to cut off the nailhead), pre-drill holes, and then hammer and set the nails.

—From the *WOOD* magazine shop

Equal—but not separated

Double-faced carpet tape works great for temporarily fastening pieces of stock together when making identical cuts such as finger joints. But, sometimes the adhesive works too well, making it nearly impossible to pull apart the pieces.

TIP: Carefully drive a narrow wedge of softwood between the two pieces. This will force them apart without marring the workpieces. If the piece still resists separation, splash lacquer thinner on the joint.

—From the *WOOD* magazine shop

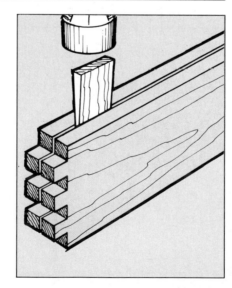

Get a grip on slippery nails

It takes the leverage of a claw hammer to remove difficult nails, but some nails slip right through the claw. If you try a different angle to grip the nail, you could mar the wood.

TIP: Clamp locking pliers over the nail shank, slide the claw under the pliers jaws, and remove the nail with ease.

—Don Butler, Waterford, Pa.

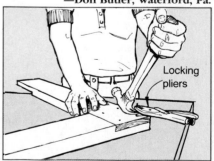

Locking pliers

Fastening and Gluing

Spin-dry your roller

We like to use paint rollers for applying white glue over large areas, such as tabletop laminations. Can the gluey roller be washed and reused?

TIP: You bet. Immediately after using it, wash it thoroughly and take this additional step:

Cut off the "business end" of an inexpensive roller frame, attach the wet roller, chuck the cut-off frame in your electric drill, and "spin-dry" the roller inside a paper bag. This effectively removes any residue left after washing, and leaves the roller nap silky smooth when dry. This trick also works when washing out latex finishes.

—From the *WOOD* magazine shop

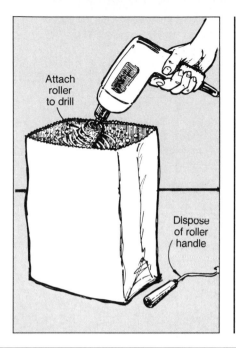

Attach roller to drill

Dispose of roller handle

Rx for difficult gluing

Getting the right amount of glue into hard-to-reach spots is a messy operation.

TIP: Inject glue with a medical syringe equipped with an 18- or 22-gauge needle. Keep the apparatus clean by flushing the syringe and needle with warm water and storing them in a closed container of water.

—From the *WOOD* magazine shop

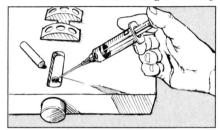

End the search for glue-bottle caps

All too often, the original cap that's supposed to seal a glue bottle vanishes from your workshop. Before you know it, your bottle spout plugs up completely with dried glue.

TIP: Electrical connectors (wire nuts), normally used to fasten and insulate electrical wires, also make excellent caps for glue bottles. Their large size and loud colors make them easy to find and keep on the bottle.

—Fred A. Race, Euclid, Ohio

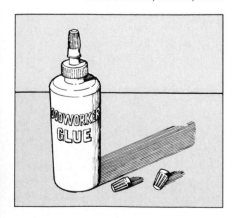

Mixing epoxy was never so easy

Many people try to match the size of two mounds of resin and hardener when mixing epoxy. This method can lead to weak, sticky bonds. The key to success: achieving correct proportions of the two materials, usually 1:1.

TIP: Run one bead of hardener next to a bead of resin of approximately the same width and length as shown *above*, and then mix together. This technique will give a ratio very close to 1:1, and consequently, a strong, durable bond.

—From the *WOOD* magazine shop

Fastening and Gluing

Tool up for straight edge gluing

Using 2×4s as flush clamp bars when gluing up boards edge to edge can easily result in misaligned boards toward the middle of the panel. The problem occurs because nontapered boards exert more pressure at the ends of the assembly than in the middle. The means to a solution: your jointer.

TIP: Mark the center of the length of a 2×4 on its face side and set the infeed table of your jointer ⅛″ below the cutterhead as illustrated in the inset drawing *below*. Lower the workpiece over the cutter at the center mark and feed it off the table so it makes a tapered cut from the middle to one end. Keep downward pressure on the infeed side of the table throughout the cut. Turn the piece end for end to make an identical cut from the center to the opposite end. This will create a clamping bar that gently bows with a central crown ⅛″ higher than its ends.

—From the *WOOD* magazine shop

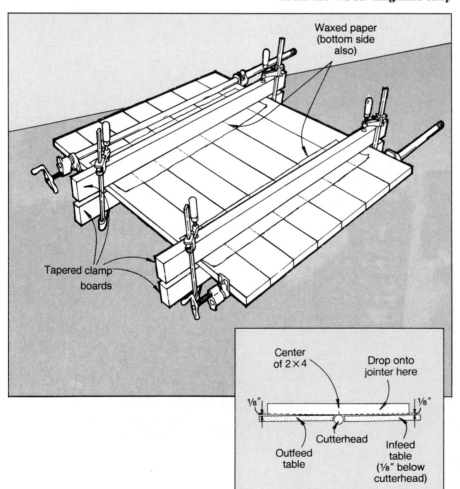

Waxed paper (bottom side also)

Tapered clamp boards

Center of 2×4

Drop onto jointer here

⅛″   ⅛″

Cutterhead

Outfeed table

Infeed table (⅛″ below cutterhead)

Repairing torn grain

No matter how skillful you are with a plane, the grain patterns of some wood species make it almost impossible to avoid raising and tearing the grain.

TIP: To fix tears, apply several drops of cyanoacrylate adhesive (the "super" variety made for wood and leather) to the affected area. Sand the spot immediately. Sanding presses the raised wood down, generates heat to set the glue, and produces fine sawdust that mixes with the glue to create an invisible and permanent repair.

—Dean Case, Nevada City, Calif.

Finish protector

Ever have a finely sanded or finished surface disfigured by just one slip of a screwdriver?

TIP: It need not happen again if you remember this trick. Simply drill a hole the exact size of the screwdriver you're using in a piece of thin stock (¼″ plywood works well for this), then clamp it in place over each hole before you begin fastening.

—From the *WOOD* magazine shop

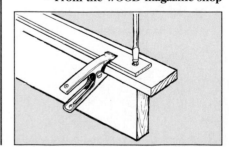

Fastening and Gluing

Putting contact cement and brushes "on hold"

Laminating large projects with contact cement often requires doing some work now and some later, with lots of mess and the loss of a dried-out brush in the course of the procedure.

TIP: Use a coffee can with a plastic lid to hold and store both cement and brush. Pour the amount of cement you think you'll be using into the can to save on mess. Cut enough off your brush handle so it fits into the can. To quit for a while, put the brush in the can. Add lacquer thinner to cover the bristles, then seal the container. Thinner keeps the brush and cement workable, but pour it off before you laminate again.

—Allan Kruger, New Port Richey, Fla.

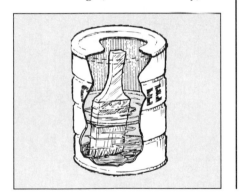

Out-of-sight nailing

Sometimes a filled nail hole stands out worse than a moose in a phone booth.

TIP: Hide that nail by using a sharp, narrow chisel or gouge to lift and turn back a small shallow flap of wood with the grain. Practice the technique on a piece of scrap of the same material first. Drive the nail inside the resulting cavity and set it. Glue and clamp the lifted section in its original position.

—From the *WOOD* magazine shop

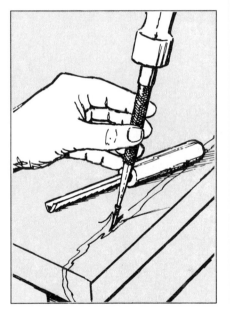

A two-faced helper you'll appreciate

It's an excellent idea to do a trial fitting of the parts of a project before tackling the permanent assembly and applying finish. A major problem with this practice is holding everything in place so later you can easily take the pieces apart.

TIP: Double-faced cellophane tape provides adequate gripping for this job and generally is easy to remove. If some of the stickiness remains after the trial assembly, wipe it away with a cloth dampened with a solvent such as acetone or lighter fluid. CAUTION: First wipe a piece of scrapwood to make sure the cleanup material doesn't stain the wood surface.

—Russell Grinolds, Owatonna, Minn.

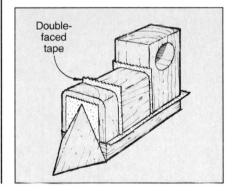

Double-faced tape

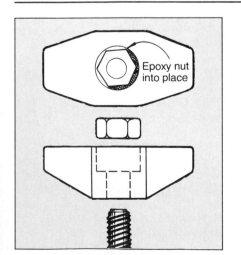

Epoxy nut into place

Custom-made wing nuts go easy on the fingers

Wing nuts can be great conveniences, but two major problems interfere with their usage:
1 Too often you have to make a special trip to the hardware store to get the size you need.
2 Those metal wings are hard on your fingers, especially if you wish to tighten the nuts securely. Sometimes, you need a pair of pliers to get the necessary leverage (which usually scratches the wing nut).

TIP: Combine a hexagonal nut and a scrap of wood to make an oversized wing nut as shown. Bore the upper hole slightly smaller than the corner-to-corner diameter of the nut and drill the lower hole for the bolt 1/64" larger than the bolt's diameter. Apply epoxy glue to the walls of the nut hole and press or tap the nut into place. This technique also works well on bolt heads.

—Paul R. Cook, Westfield, N.Y.

Fastening and Gluing

Keep threads open when cutting bolts

Occasionally, it's necessary to cut off a bolt that's too long for a specific job. Hacksawing the bolt usually closes the threads, making it very hard—if not impossible—to start the nut.

TIP: Thread on a wing nut before sawing the bolt, then grind the sawed end on a grinding wheel or belt sander, rotating the bolt 360°. Now the wing nut, which aids in holding the bolt during grinding, will help open the threads completely when spun off. If the wing nut doesn't spin off with little effort, grind the bolt until you can easily remove it.

—From the *WOOD* magazine shop

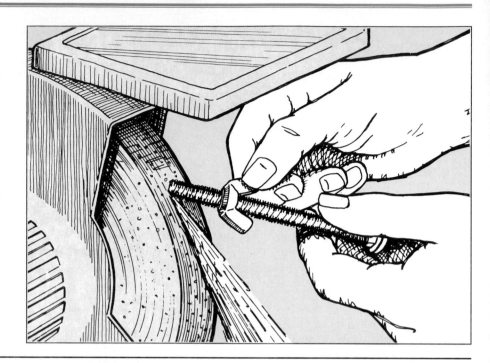

Work smarter alone

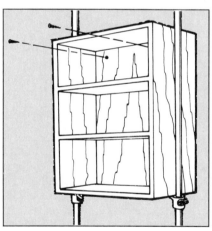

There's usually no getting around it: Some tasks, such as hanging wall-mounted cabinets, simply require at least one helper. Unfortunately, often the work is ready to be mounted but the trusty assistant cannot be found anywhere.

TIP: Use long pipe clamps as shown *above* to support the load as you drill the necessary holes and drive the screws.

—From the *WOOD* magazine shop

A tip goes "full cycle"

Ouch! Extended use of a hammer or screwdriver locates hand muscles you never knew you had. Blisters may also result from steady activity.

TIP: To cushion your hand from aches and blisters, wear bicycling gloves. The padded palm cushions blows. Because the gloves are fingerless, it's still easy to pick up and hold hardware, nails, and tools.

—David Williams, Cheraw, S.C.

Installing brads in a pinch

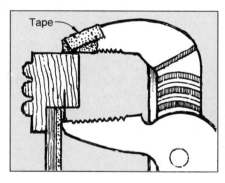

It's not easy to hammer brads into a picture frame to hold the backing in place. Of course, you could buy a framemaker's brad-setting tool. But they're expensive for such an infrequent task.

TIP: Common slip-joint "water pump" pliers make a good substitute for a brad-setting tool. To prevent marring, wrap five or six layers of masking tape around the jaw that will contact the frame. Then slowly and steadily squeeze the brad into the frame, as shown in the drawing *above*.

—Van Caldwell, Cincinnati

Fastening and Gluing

No soap

Yuck! You use a bar of soap to lubricate wood screws, but it's a mess keeping the soap damp. In addition, soap can cause rusting.

TIP: Try using toilet-bowl wax gasket seals. The wax is ideal for lubricating screws and nails. It will not attract moisture and can be purchased at your local hardware store.

—Max Beard, Silver Spring, Md.

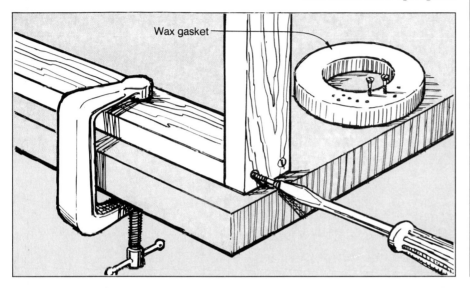

Wax gasket

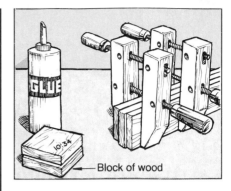

Block of wood

Time's up

Most of us forget to note the time when projects are glued and clamped. Unfortunately, the clamps are often removed before the glue has set.

TIP: After you apply the clamps, glue two scraps of wood together (don't clamp them), and jot down the time. When these scraps are set, the clamped wood also will be set.

—From the *WOOD* magazine shop

Cooling eager epoxy

Sometimes epoxy cement begins to set up before you're through using a batch. This is most likely to be a problem when you're working in a warm place or during hot weather.

TIP: Extend the set-up time of epoxy by keeping it cool. One successful way to do this is to mix the ingredients in the recess in the bottom of a chilled can of soft drink. When finished gluing, return the pop to the refrigerator or open it and have a cool, refreshing break.

—Rich Webb, Grand Island, Neb.

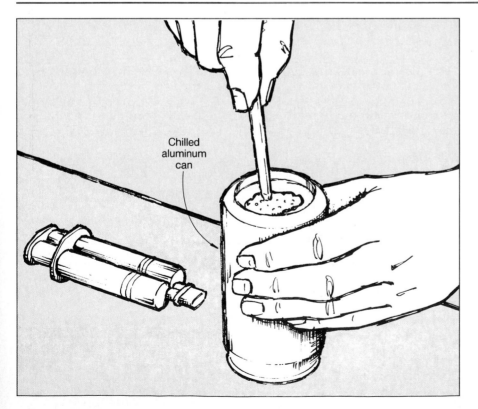

Chilled aluminum can

Fastening and Gluing

Make fast work of laminating

Applying plastic laminate to two faces of a cabinet door, shelf, or other stock eats up a lot of your time when you do one side first, then wait for it to dry before covering the second side.

TIP: You can apply the laminate to both sides almost simultaneously. First, drive brads or small finishing nails into the corners of the stock, as shown *below*. Apply contact cement to this side and then turn over the stock so the nails support it. Now, apply cement to the other face and to the two pieces of laminate you have prefit. Allow the cement to dry until tacky, and place the first piece of laminate on the side without nails. Flip the stock over, pull out the nails with pliers, and carefully lay the second sheet of laminate into position. Allow the cement to cure.

—Roy T. Higa, Honolulu

Finish nail
CONTACT CEMENT

Take the slip out of slick glue

When you apply pressure to boards or sheet goods that you're attempting to surface-laminate, the stack wants to slide around.

TIP: To prevent this from happening, drive wire brads into the material before applying the glue. Snip off the brad head at a sharp diagonal. Now apply glue and, after aligning the boards, tap them together with a mallet.

—C.P. Squires, Warrensville, N.C.

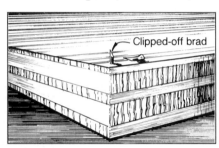

Clipped-off brad

Tight-squeeze tweezers

Do you have trouble getting a grip on tiny fasteners, especially when trying to install them in tight spots?

TIP: Try these homemade tweezers. To make them, mount a bobby pin in the end of a 6″ length of 5/16″ dowel. Drill a ¼″ deep hole in one end of the dowel, then force the looped end of the pin into the hole. If needed, secure the pin with a few drops of epoxy.

—Charles Whatley, Cincinnati

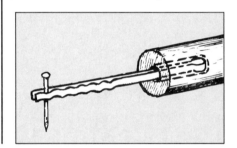

A gripping idea for nail removal

You can almost count on the wood splitting when you attempt to pull a finish nail from wood trim or molding you wish to recycle.

TIP: Pull these nails through the back side by bending the shank over slightly so your claw hammer can grab it more easily.

Even better, grip the shank of the nail with the jaws of a diagonal wire cutter, slip the hammer claw between the wood and the cutters, and pry out the nail.

—Myron S. Levy, Gold Hill, Ore.

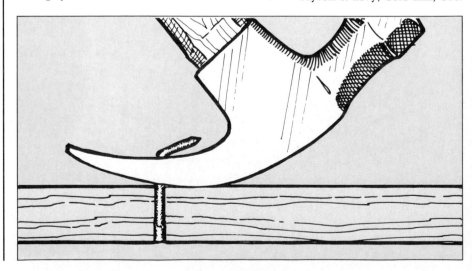

Fastening and Gluing

Save that carpet scrap for applying adhesive

You might as well throw away a brush after using it to spread contact cement on a project. It makes a hopeless cleanup job.

TIP: Don't waste your time or materials on cleanup when working with contact cement. A clean scrap of carpet wrapped around a block of wood spreads the glue evenly. Toss the carpet when finished.

—**From the *WOOD* magazine shop**

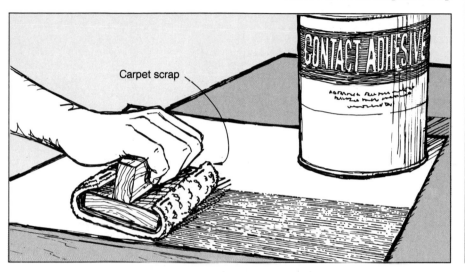

Carpet scrap

CONTACT ADHESIVE

Offset screwdriver reaches tight spots

Sometimes you have to drive a screw in an area where there simply isn't enough room to use a conventional screwdriver.

TIP: You can buy a bounty of screwdriver tips these days, including slotted, Phillips, square, Torx, and other bits. For an offset screwdriver, insert the appropriate bit in a ¼″ socket or ratchet wrench and proceed. Single-tipped bits work best.

—**Ron Odegaard, Appleton, Wis.**

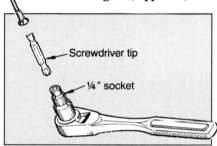

Screwdriver tip

¼″ socket

Toothpick magic

Rarely can you find the right size small pieces of wood around your shop for the array of small gluing tasks.

TIP: Pick up a box of flat toothpicks for your workshop—you'll be amazed at how helpful they can be to you.

A toothpick is handy for spreading glue and working glue into tight cracks. Toothpicks also make a world of difference when you glue them into loose screw holes. Fill a slightly off-center screw hole with a toothpick and glue, allow to dry, and then drill a new screw hole on the edge of the original hole. These handy minitimbers can also fill old nail holes in salvaged lumber; leave the ends long and sand smooth after the glue dries.

—**E.R. Huckleberry, Salt Lake City**

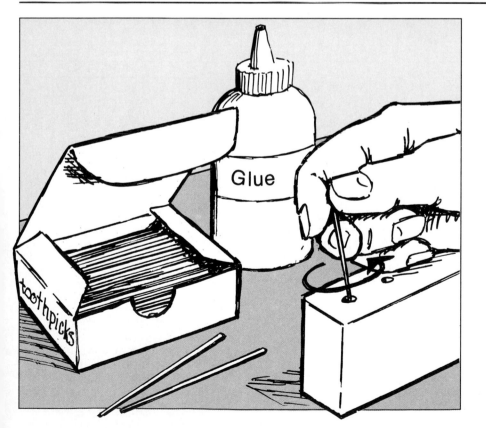

Glue

toothpicks

Fastening and Gluing

Handy lubricant storage

When driving a nail the wood often splits. The same happens if you drive screws without drilling pilot holes first.

TIP: Coat nails with beeswax or paraffin before nailing. Rubbing lubricant into the threads of wood screws makes them easier to set. Also, keep lubricant handy by storing it in a 3/8"-diameter × 3/4"-deep hole drilled in the hammer handle. Melt beeswax or paraffin on a stove, then pour it into the hole.

—**From the *WOOD* magazine shop**

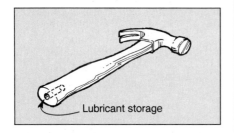

Lubricant storage

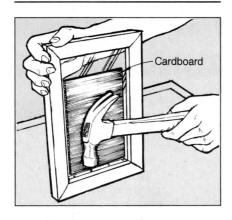

Cardboard

Protect your glass

If you're not careful, nailing the stops into a picture frame can be a shattering experience.

TIP: You'll have a better chance of keeping the glass intact if you tape a piece of thin cardboard over it before nailing in the stops. Hold the hammer lightly against the cardboard and slide it up and down to drive the nail.

—**From the *WOOD* magazine shop**

Catching telltale glue splotches before they tattle

All too often, you don't notice spots of glue film on your project until after you've started to apply the stain or finish.

TIP: You can show up those little smears by wiping all joints and adjacent areas with mineral spirits or lacquer thinner. The glue smears will remain light-colored but the surrounding wood will darken when wetted. Be careful not to soak the wood with solvent.

—**Frederick Schramm, Magalia, Calif.**

Glue

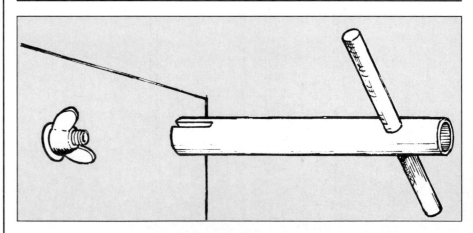

How to loosen stubborn wing nuts

A tight wing nut can chew up fingers before you get it loosened.

TIP: Make a wrench out of a 12" length of 1/2"-diameter electrical conduit and a 4" length of 1/4" steel rod. Cut notches 3/16" wide and 1/2" deep in one end of the conduit. About 3/4" from the opposite end, drill a 1/4" hole, insert the steel rod, and glue in place with epoxy.

—**Lloyd T. Murphy, Oak Ridge, Tenn.**

Fastening and Gluing

Getting that darned knob attached

Some wood isn't thick enough to drill into to hold a knob like the one shown here. Or worse yet, you can't start a screw through the back of the dimensional lumber.

TIP: Make your own hanger bolts to secure the knob. First install a sheet-metal screw into the knob (try a 2½" or 3" No. 8 screw). Then saw off the head of the screw and grind the top to a point. Drill a hole in the drawer or door and fasten them together.

—Marion L. Adams, New Salisbury, Ind.

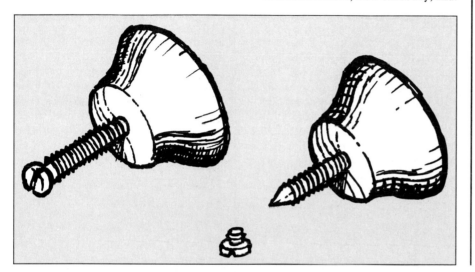

A thread in time

Threaded inserts make great fasteners, but there just has to be an easier way to install them.

TIP: There is! Match a machine bolt to the size of the inner threads of the insert. Thread two nuts on the end of the bolt and tighten them against each other. Screw in the insert with a ratchet and back out the machine bolt. (*We found that a drill press works even better—Ed.*)

—J.O. Atkinson, Pioneer, Calif.

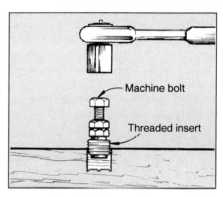

Machine bolt

Threaded insert

Yet another use for those plastic jugs

Epoxy is a great adhesive, but the glue left in the mixing container is impossible to remove.

TIP: The versatile one-gallon milk jug comes to the rescue again. Cut out a section of the bottle and mix the glue in the container. When the leftover glue has cured, bend the flexible jug and you'll be able to pop out the residue.

—From the *WOOD* magazine shop

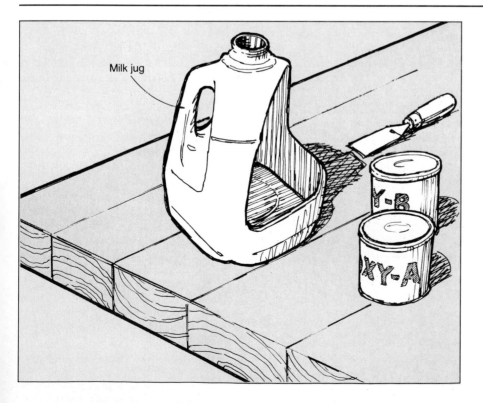

Milk jug

Finishing and Refinishing

Great way to store brushes between coats

Between finishing coats, it would be nice if you didn't have to thoroughly clean the brush. You could place the brush in a jar filled with thinner, but that oftens damages the bristles.

TIP: Recycle a container from disposable wet wiping cloths (sometimes called "baby wipes") for use as a temporary brush container. The slits in the cover form a snug opening and suspend the brush in solvent without bending the bristles. Some solvents will dissolve plastic containers, so check by placing a small amount of the solvent in the container.

—Daniel Borken, Bloomington, Minn.

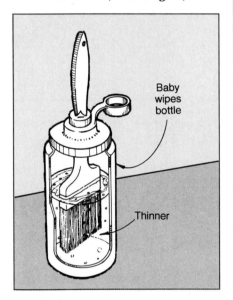

Baby wipes bottle

Thinner

Aerosol touch-up trick

Touching up small areas with aerosol paints can be touchy. If you aim the spray at one spot, the paint globs on the surface.

TIP: Through the center of a folded newspaper, cut a hole the size of the spot to be sprayed and center the hole over the spot, as shown *below*. Peak the fold slightly above the surface, and make several quick spraying passes across the hole. The moving spray prevents paint from accumulating in one spot, and the raised paper allows some of the residual spray to creep beneath the edges and feather out over the surface.

—**From the *WOOD* magazine shop**

Tear hole in paper

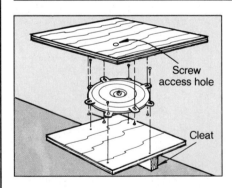

Screw access hole

Cleat

World-champion finishing jig

Applying aerosol paint, polyurethane, or any other finish to more than one side of an object is an awkward, messy chore.

TIP: A steel swivel made to support a boxer's punching bag makes an ideal shop aid for holding objects that need finishing. Attach the swivel to a secure overhead support, screw an eyehook into the object to be finished, and hang the piece on the swivel. The workpiece—not the woodworker—does all the moving. (A plant hanger that swivels is an inexpensive alternative for working with lightweight objects.)

—Tony Bofinger, Punxsutawney, Pa.

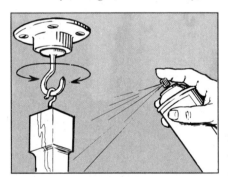

A handy lazy Susan for large finishing tasks

Moving around your big projects while finishing can become bothersome and tiring.

TIP: A turntable allows you to stand in one spot and move the work into range. From ¾" plywood, cut pieces measuring 24×24" and 15×15". Fasten a 6" ball-bearing heavy-duty lazy Susan fixture (available at many hardware stores) to the bottom of the larger piece. Then, fasten this assembly to the smaller piece. Add a 2×4×15" cleat to the center to secure the turntable in a vise.

—George A. Heffelfinger, Lehighton, Pa.

Finishing and Refinishing

Piggyback brush holder

You're brushing paint or varnish on your project, when the phone or doorbell rings. Where's a clean place to put the brush?

TIP: Use masking tape or duct tape to attach a small plastic container to the outside of the paint or varnish can. Narrow, oval, or rectangular containers work best in this situation.

—Jeff Mathers, Grimes, Iowa

Plastic container with top cut off

Collapsible varnish storage

Partially filled varnish cans tend to "skin over" quickly.

TIP: Pour the remaining unused varnish into a plastic, bellows-type container obtainable from photographic equipment suppliers; it allows you to squeeze out any air that's inside before capping. The less air, the less reaction and "skin over."

—From the *WOOD* magazine shop

WOOD FINISH

Second wind for clogged aerosols

Inverting and spraying an aerosol can to clear paint material from the nozzle never seems absolutely necessary—until it's time to use the spray can again. Now what can you do?

TIP: Remove plugged spray-can nozzles and boil them in water for a few minutes. Air bubbles that have been trapped in the paint or other coating material will be forced through the system, clearing the nozzle.

—From the *WOOD* magazine shop

No-strain brush cleaning

Cleaning paint and varnish brushes in previously used solvent often stirs up dirty sludge at the bottom of the can.

TIP: Don't throw away that used solvent. You can save it by making a basket from screen wire or using a small kitchen strainer to keep your brushes from touching the paint residue. Secure the wire around the lip of the container; the basket should extend at least 3″ into the solvent. To speed the cleaning, scrub bristles against the wire. After you've finished a project, strain the solvent through the wire mesh and store the solvent in a clean, tightly covered container.

—Vernon A Daily, Wills Point, Texas

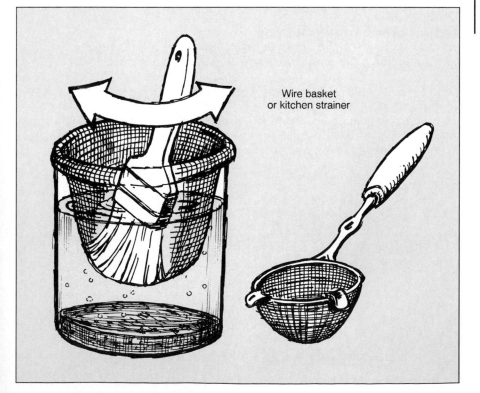

Wire basket or kitchen strainer

Finishing and Refinishing

Applying finishes smoothly

Uniform coats are the exception rather than the rule with some brushable finishes.

TIP: To apply lacquers and polyurethane finishes smoothly, fill a pan with hot tap water, and set the can of finish in it for a few minutes before use. Raising the material's temperature by only a few degrees—and choosing a polyurethane foam brush as an applicator—will help you achieve a pleasing, uniform look when the finish dries.

—From the *WOOD* magazine shop

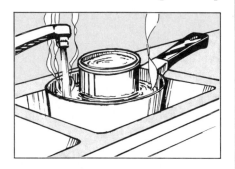

Paintbrush maintenance

Your paintbrush is clean but not dry. What's a good way to remove water or paint thinner so you can use the brush again?

TIP: Hold the brush between your palms and spin it back and forth vigorously. Centrifugal force will spin away excess moisture and fluff out the bristles—which helps prevent the brush from drying into an unmanageable lump.

—From the *WOOD* magazine shop

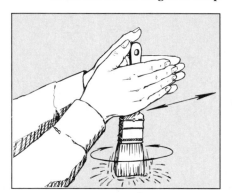

Soft touch with stain

Using a paintbrush to apply oil-based stains works well enough, but cleaning the brushes afterward takes time and wastes paint thinner.

TIP: Use scraps of foam rubber as stain applicators. You can buy leftovers at crafts stores for pennies and cut pieces just the size and shape to fit the staining job. The foam rubber reaches into corners and cracks while your hands stay clean. When finished, discard the applicator and move onto something more productive than cleanup.

—Thornton H. Waite, Idaho Falls, Idaho

Airtight storage

Those little foam brushes are great, but they dry out and become brittle between coats.

TIP: Store them for the second coat in zipper-locking plastic freezer bags. The bags are airtight, so they will keep the brushes pliable until needed.

—From the *WOOD* magazine shop

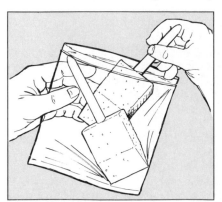

Tight-squeeze brush cleaning

Because so much paint and varnish remain in a brush after it's been used, a lot of expensive solvents wind up being wasted.

TIP: More effective than wiping your brush on a scrap piece of wood or cardboard is trapping paint or varnish between several layers of newspaper or magazine pages. Use finger pressure to squeeze the bristles while you withdraw the brush. Use mineral spirits or your favorite brush cleaner to remove the remaining paint or varnish.

—Walt Morrison, Northport, N.Y.

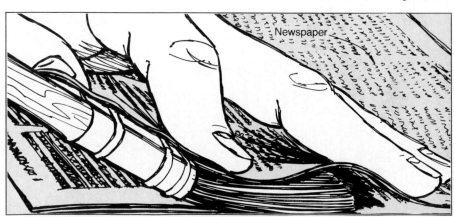

Finishing and Refinishing

Pinstripe like a pro

Using short strokes, it's practically impossible to paint a neat pinstripe of consistent width on a wheel or other circular object.

TIP: First, attach the object to its actual axle or a temporary one. Then, with your hand resting in a fixed position, slowly rotate the wheel and apply the stripe with the brush at a right angle to the wheel. Be sure to use a good brush and practice both thinning the paint to a suitable viscosity and handling the brush. The paint must be thin enough to flow, but not run.

—James Wilhoit, Aiken, S.C.

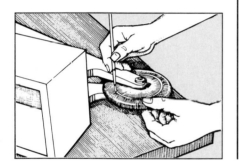

Put some heat on tape so it releases cleanly

Applying masking tape to glass before finishing or painting frames makes cleaning up quick and easy. The hitch: removing the tape. Once it's been in place for a few days, the adhesive clings to the pane so tightly that the tape tears when you try to pull it up.

TIP: Use a hand-held hair dryer to warm the tape slightly beforehand and it will peel off cleanly without tearing.

—Ray Ferreri, Stormville, N.Y.

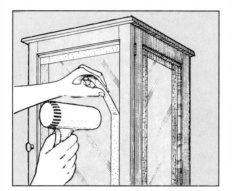

Put a bib on messy contact cement cans

Drippings from your brush can quickly coat the rim of a container of contact cement and dry, making it practically impossible to put the lid back on tightly. A poor seal will allow air to leak in and harden the remaining cement.

TIP: Form a piece of aluminum foil into place as a bib along at least half of the can's rim. This will catch the inevitable overflow of glue from your brush, preventing rim gum-up.

—James Moffat, Allentown, Pa.

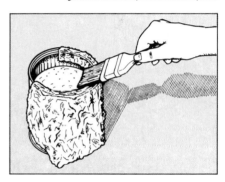

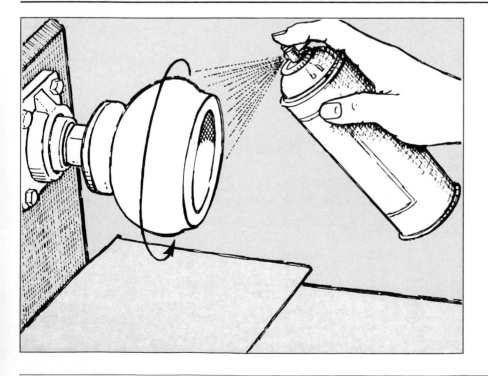

Light coat of finish lets you clearly see defects

In the final stages of sanding a turning project, minor scratches in the surface can be practically impossible to detect. It's really disappointing to start applying the finishing material only to discover imperfections you missed earlier.

TIP: With an aerosol finish, spray on a light coat while the piece rotates on your lathe. This will quickly reveal hard-to-see faults such as fine scratches and chip-outs along glued joints when working them out is still fairly simple. Also, you may want to use a piece of cardboard to catch the overspray and protect your equipment.

—From the *WOOD* magazine shop

Finishing and Refinishing

Swab idea for coating hard-to-reach spots

You can pull on your ear for a long time before figuring out how to flood stain, varnish, or paint into holes and crevices missed with a brush.

TIP: Cotton swabs are ideal for getting finish or glue into tight areas. The cotton holds an amazing amount of liquid to make fast work of small jobs. And better yet, swabs are inexpensive and disposable.

—Fred Whetzel, Elizabethtown, Ky.

Stripping irregular shapes

How do you get the old finish out of ornate carvings and details on furniture that you're stripping while preserving your sanity and the wood?

TIP: Wear rubber gloves and use a handful of sawdust or coarse wood chips as a scrubber to remove the stripper and old finish from difficult spots. The chips' scouring action takes off the softened finish without damaging the wood.

—From the *WOOD* magazine shop

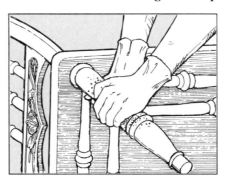

No-skin varnish storage

If you allow a skin to form over varnish, paint, or other finish stored in partially used cans, you're throwing money and material down the drain.

TIP: Put a layer of kitchen-type plastic wrap on the surface of the liquid, pressing its edges against the sides of the can. You want to make sure that little or no air is trapped between the surface of the finish and the plastic wrap.

—Lloyd Murphy, Oak Ridge, Tenn.

A curtain call for finishing small parts

Finding a suitable place to keep small parts while they dry can leave you in a real quandary.

TIP: Screw a length of curtain rod to a ceiling joist for a great out-of-the-way place to hang up such parts. Slip drapery carriers into the track, add curtain hooks, and you have a drying rack that's ready to use. Screw small cup hooks into the backs of the workpieces and hang them on the rack with lengths of wire or thread and apply finish. These will hold a surprising amount of weight. If you don't want to make screw holes in the backs of the pieces, use straight pins with hooks bent into them near the heads. Or, attach hooks with hotmelt adhesive.

—Robert McGloin, Elyria, Ohio

Finishing and Refinishing

Cut painting time in half

Problems arise when you need to paint or finish the second side of a project. You can either wait for one surface to dry before turning the piece over, or you can finish both sides the same day and expect a lot of touch-up on the side painted first.

TIP: Drive ¾" brads through scraps of ½" wood. Arrange three or more of these spacers on your work surface, turn the piece over, and continue painting on a horizontal surface. Save and reuse blocks of wood later.

—James C. Hunt, Southgate, Mich.

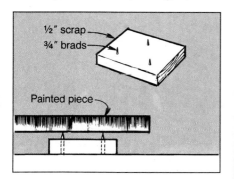

½" scrap
¾" brads
Painted piece

Pour an inside finish

Sometimes, it's impossible to use paintbrushes to apply finishes to the inside of small hollow objects such as vases.

TIP: For these occasions, it's easier and more effective to pour finish into the hollow article, turn and tilt to coat all surfaces adequately, and then pour out the finishing material. Be sure to invert the piece long enough to drain completely.

—From the *WOOD* magazine shop

Start out clean

Nozzles on paint sprayers are difficult to get thoroughly clean. Many times, dried residue clogs the nozzle and sends paint spitting around the room.

TIP: Clean the nozzle as best you can after use, then store it submerged in fresh thinner in the sprayer's container. Before you start your next spraying job, pour out the thinner, and enjoy one less frustration.

—From the *WOOD* magazine shop

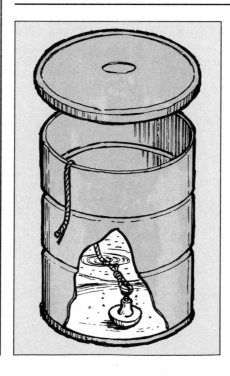

Nylon-smooth finish

Polyurethane makes a great finish for many projects, but cleaning brushes after use often takes longer than applying the finish. And with quick-drying products, brush marks can also be a problem on some surfaces.

TIP: Ask someone to save you a few pairs of discarded nylon stockings or panty hose. Cut the hose into 6" long strips and use the wadded strips to apply finish. Dispose of the strip after use. No brushes to clean and you get a "nylon-smooth" finish with no streaks or brush marks.

—From the *WOOD* magazine shop

Nylon stocking

Stripping small parts: leave 'em hanging

Stripping finish from small parts, such as drawer pulls, is time-consuming and wastes a lot of finish remover.

TIP: Remove the part from the workpiece, replace the screw, and tie a 12" length of string around the screw. Fill a coffee can with enough stripper to cover the part. Drop the part into the can, hang the string over the edge, and cover the can with the plastic lid. Soak and clean as recommended in the refinisher instructions. You can reuse the stripper over and over.

—Tom Brower, Northboro, Mass.

Finishing and Refinishing

Give tough stripping problems the brush-off

When refinishing furniture, working the stripper into tight corners and finely detailed work can prove hard work. Brass brushes help, but cost money, too, and may damage the wood if used too vigorously.

TIP: Scrub away the loosened finish from intricate carvings, deep grain, and other hard-to-get areas with an old paintbrush. First, cut off the bristles to a length of 1″ to make them stiff enough to work nicely. For best results, generously dab on the stripper without overbrushing it during application.

—Mark Ceola, Fayetteville, Ark.

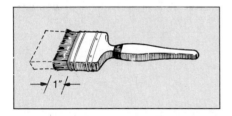

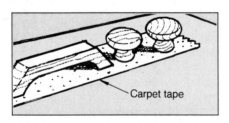
Carpet tape

Finish goes on small parts— not your fingers

Applying practically any kind of finish to small wooden pieces often turns into a messy process. Whether you spray or brush the finish, keeping the parts in one place can be difficult.

TIP: You'll find it a snap to finish small items such as knobs and pulls if you press them onto strips of double-faced cloth-backed carpet tape attached to a sheet of corrugated cardboard.

—Dixie Thorne, Ojai, Calif.

See the light and make finishing easier

Despite paying careful attention, it's easy to overlook an area when you apply finish coats with a brush or sprayer.

TIP: Use a table lamp or some type of portable lighting unit to inspect the finish while it's still wet. Viewed from approximately a 45° angle to the surface, the properly brushed or sprayed area will glisten in the light. Dull areas indicate the spots where you need to apply additional finish.

—From the *WOOD* magazine shop

How to come out a winner in the mixing game

Hand-mixing paints, stains, and powdered wood fillers, can be tedious and time-consuming. And often, the stirring attachments made for electric drills provide either too much or too little agitation for the amount of material you're mixing.

TIP: For your next mixing job, chuck a beater from an electric kitchen mixer into a variable-speed drill. Start mixing slowly, then increase the speed until you get a feel for how the beater works. You can buy cheap beaters in various sizes from flea markets and secondhand stores.

—Greg Howard, Bremerton, Wash.

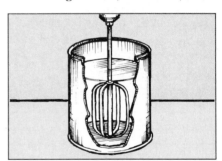

Put the squeeze on tung oil

There's nothing more exasperating than discovering that the tung oil you've saved has solidified into an unusable mass in a partially filled container.

TIP: Recycled shampoo bottles with a flip-up spout are excellent for storing tung oil and other finishes. Thoroughly rinse and dry shampoo bottles before filling them with finish. Squeeze excess air from the bottle and flip the spout closed. Be sure to label the contents of the bottle with an indelible marker, and transfer any safety warnings from the original container to the shampoo bottle.

—Ross G. Roepke, Tullahoma, Tenn.

Finishing and Refinishing

How to win the stain game

You've played this guessing game before—how is a given stain going to turn out on the particular wood you're using?

TIP: Cut a fairly good-sized piece of scrap or cut-off stock from your project. Sand it smooth, then divide the piece into several sections. As you test stains to see what they really look like (either from your shop paint shelf or from the store—many dealers will share a small sample), identify the type used in each section.

—**Bill Blakeney, Lincoln, Del.**

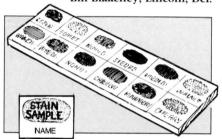

Fuzz buster

How many times have you smoothly finished new wood, only to have the grain raised by stain, paint, or varnish? You've got a bad case of fuzz, friend.

TIP: Before you apply the first coat of finish, wipe down the entire project with a damp sponge or cloth. Allow the wood to dry, then remove all the fuzz with fine steel wool or sandpaper. (Be sure to use a clean tack cloth to remove dust before applying stain or finish to ensure smooth results.)

—**From the *WOOD* magazine shop**

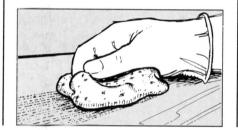

Eliminate "sticky feet" when finishing

When varnishing, applying lacquer to, or painting furniture, the wet finish often runs down the legs and makes them stick to the floor or workbench. Pulling them loose can damage your project and/or work surface.

TIP: Eliminate this nuisance by placing flat metal washers under the ends of the legs. If any excess finish accumulates, it's at the end of the leg where it can be sanded away without harming the workpiece.

—**From the *WOOD* magazine shop**

A finishing record you'll never misplace

You've been successful with a lot of finishing techniques and products, but the combination of finishes used on an individual piece of furniture often escapes your mind. What was it that you used on that great-looking cherry table or oak chair? Hmmm?

TIP: If you sample many different products, it's especially important to note your comments right on the project. Before finishing (or refinishing), apply peel-and-stick labels or glue paper to an inconspicuous area of the project. Note the date and any important facts about how you did it. The finish you apply over the paper will guarantee that you can refer to your notes in the future.

—**Ralph Briggs, Des Moines**

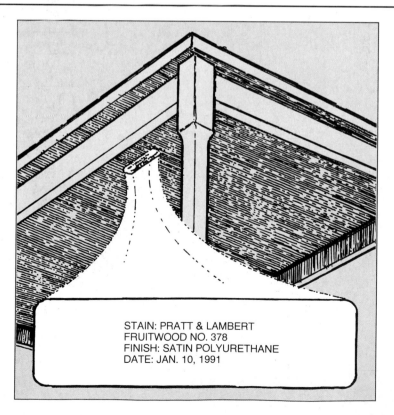

STAIN: PRATT & LAMBERT
FRUITWOOD NO. 378
FINISH: SATIN POLYURETHANE
DATE: JAN. 10, 1991

Furniture Repair

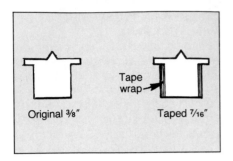

Original 3/8″ Taped 7/16″

Tape wrap

Fitting dowel centers to those "odd" repairs

When repairing old furniture, you often run across odd-size dowels and dowel holes, such as 7/16″, for example. What do you do if your dowel center set has none for that size?

TIP: Using the next smaller size dowel center, wrap electrical tape around it as shown in the drawing at *left*. Wrap the tape carefully and evenly, so the point remains centered. Stop wrapping the center when it fits snugly in the hole.

—Dan Miller, Elgin, Ill.

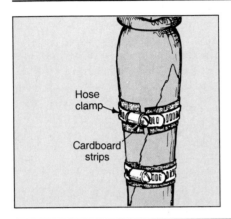

Hose clamp

Cardboard strips

Putting the squeeze on broken legs

The conventional way of fixing breaks in cylindrical furniture legs often seems like more trouble than it's worth: building a jig to hold the leg, then gluing and clamping it with a C-clamp.

TIP: You can do the job just as well—and much faster—with stainless-steel hose clamps as shown in the drawing at *left.* You'll find a wide variety of sizes at most auto-supply stores. To avoid marring the piece when tightening the clamps, insert a strip of cardboard between the clamp and the work.

—Hal Doolittle, Kirkwood, Mo.

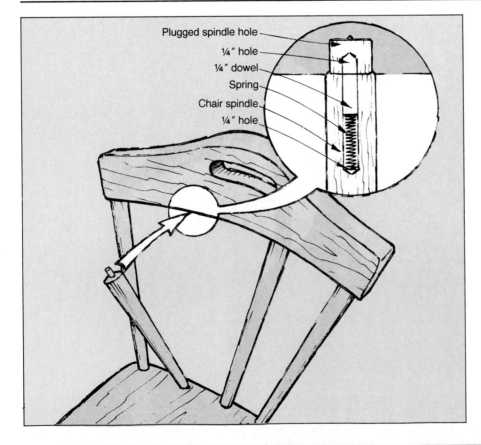

Plugged spindle hole
1/4″ hole
1/4″ dowel
Spring
Chair spindle
1/4″ hole

Easy spindle repair saves you from disassembly

The rung in the back of a chair or a stretcher between chair legs may break, even though all the chair's joints remain tight.

TIP: Turn a replacement part or use the old one if it can be repaired. You may need to shorten one tenon so you can wiggle the damaged piece into the original position. Drill a 1/4″ hole into the center of the shortened tenon deep enough to accept a 2″-long dowel and a ballpoint pen spring. Next, bore a 1/4″ hole at least 1/2″ deep into the middle of the plugged spindle hole as shown in the drawing at *left.* Apply glue to both ends of the rung and slip into place as you would reload a roll of toilet paper. The spring will push the dowel into place and, when the glue sets, the dowel will make the repair permanent.

—Earl W. Zieg, Fairfax, Va.

Furniture Repair

The once-and-for-all cure for wobbly chairs

Despite your best efforts to make a lasting repair, a troublesome screw continues to loosen on a wobbly chair.

TIP: Remove the screw and dip the threads in epoxy, then reinstall and allow it to dry. (Epoxy has more holding power than woodworker's glue.) If the screw hole has worn too large, use toothpicks or slivers of wood to help fill the opening.

—From the *WOOD* magazine shop

Stripped, but not forgotten

When a wood screw is stripped of its holding power, it seems that nothing can back it out of its hole.

TIP: Driving small finish nails from different angles into the screw, as shown in the drawing *below,* is the first step to defeating the troublemaker. The nails provide you with enough bite to back the screw out, and you can grab the head with your fingers or pliers.

—Edwin M. Dery, Monticello, Fla.

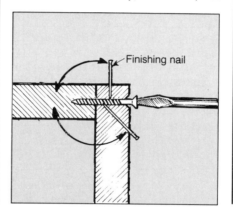

Quick cure for wobbly joints

Although the size of most mortise or dowel holes remains the same, wood fitting into the joint often shrinks over the years and creates a loose fit in furniture.

TIP: Use a piece of linen or sheet between the wooden parts. Coat the cloth and hole liberally with glue. After you fit the pieces together, wipe off the excess glue with a damp rag, and trim the unneeded cloth with a knife or razor blade.

—Larry Bedaw, North Swanzey, N.H.

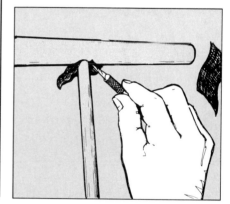

Easy does it

Taking furniture apart for regluing often requires breaking a sturdy glue bond. Improperly done, too much pressure can damage the pieces.

TIP: Pop apart glued joints by applying inside pressure with an inexpensive device you can make at home. Continuous-thread rod, sometimes called all-thread, is the key to this mechanism. Drill a hole for the rod through two blocks of wood and then line one side of each block with carpet or foam as shown at *right.* To apply even pressure and break the bond without damage to the workpiece, just tighten the washer and nut inside each block.

—Donald F. Kinnaman, Phoenix

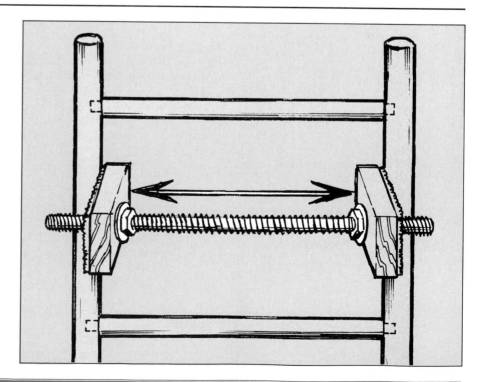

Furniture Repair

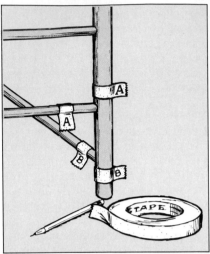

Fitting the pieces back together

After completely taking apart a chair for regluing, all the legs and rungs suddenly look alike. And just as suddenly, you have an assembly problem as tough as any jigsaw puzzle.

TIP: Before taking the chair apart, label all the parts with numbered or lettered masking tape. After you clean the joint, use your identification system to correctly glue and reassemble. When the glue dries and the clamps are removed, peel off tape markers.

—John Paul Christopher, North Kansas City, Mo.

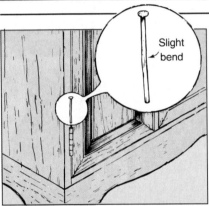

Bent on success

Well-used hinges have a tendency to loosen with age. If the problem goes unchecked, some doors won't close properly.

TIP: A bent hinge pin makes a lot of difference in how an old hinge operates. Tap the pin slightly in the center to create a bend. The hinge should open and close with a smoother action.

—From the *WOOD* magazine shop

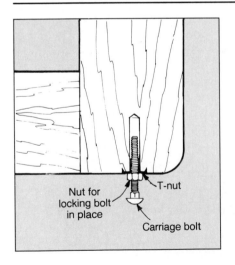

On the level

Do your tables and benches have the wobbles? Corrective leveling hardware can be expensive and sometimes hard to find.

TIP: Save money by making your own leveling hardware from T-nuts, carriage bolts, and nuts. Drill the holes for the T-nut deep enough to accept half or more of the carriage bolt, as shown at *left*. After leveling the table, tighten the nut to lock the bolt in place.

—Stephen Cabiroy, Ballston Spa, N.Y.

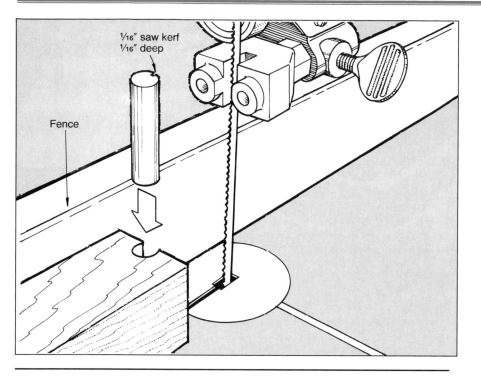

1/16" saw kerf
1/16" deep

Fence

A simple jig for grooving dowels

Carefully fitted dowels will trap both air and excess glue when inserted. Unless you provide an escape route, that air or adhesive may prevent you from bringing together the joined pieces. If you force them together, the built-up hydraulic pressure may cause the dowel to pop out of its hole when you're not looking.

TIP: For dowels 1½" to 2" long, build a jig out of scrapwood as thick as the dowel length. Near one end, drill a hole the same diameter as the dowel and then crosscut the scrap so two-thirds of the hole remains as shown at *left*. Insert the dowel in the jig and cut a 1/16" saw kerf 1/16" deep with a bandsaw or scroll-saw. One groove will allow air and glue to escape. Now, you can plug away with confidence in your doweled joints!

—George Mitro, Jr., El Paso, Texas

No more rattles

Drawer bottoms must remain free-floating (not glued to the drawer frame) to allow for expansion and contraction due to changes in humidity. But often the bottom will develop a rattle as the drawer parts loosen up.

TIP: Apply a fillet of silicone sealer along the dadoed joints where the bottom fits into the frame. The flexible silicone silences the rattle, yet allows the drawer to expand and contract as it needs to.

—From the *WOOD* magazine shop

Plugs with pizzazz

Normally, you want flush dowel plugs to be unobtrusive and not noticed. But if that's not possible, why not make them real eye-catchers?

TIP: To make attention-grabbing plugs, laminate several layers of contrasting veneers between the halves of a hardwood block, as shown *below*. After the glue dries, use a plug cutter and cut plugs with real zip. Or, use just one contrasting color to simulate traditional wedged plugs.

—Timothy Breidenbach, Grand Forks, N.D.

Let trapped air and glue escape dowel holes

If you only occasionally use dowels, and want a means of kerfing them that's simpler than the tip given above, stay tuned.

TIP: Place the dowel in your woodworking vise and with a thin-kerf blade, saw a 1/16"-deep groove to provide an air/glue escape route. Rest the saw against the vise jaw to control the cut as shown *below*.

—From the *WOOD* magazine shop

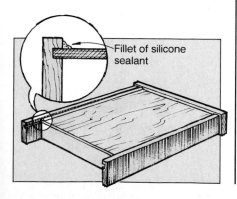

Fillet of silicone sealant

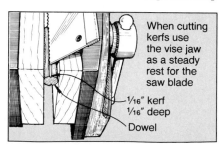

When cutting kerfs use the vise jaw as a steady rest for the saw blade

1/16" kerf
1/16" deep

Dowel

Joinery

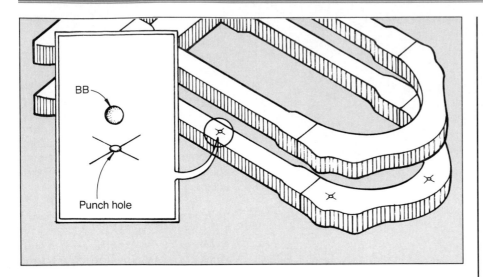

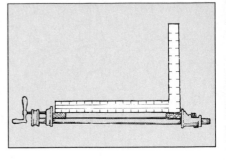

BBs hit bull's-eye for dowel-hole placement

Precisely locating dowel holes in matching pieces with curved shapes will help you produce a properly fitted project. Here's a method that's quicker and just as accurate as using small nails as described in the quilt rack project in the February 1987 issue of WOOD *magazine.*

TIP: First, mark the centerpoints of the dowels with an awl. Then, tap BBs slightly into each awl mark. Place the corresponding curved top piece precisely on top of the first one and tap with a rubber mallet. When you separate the two wood pieces, the BBs will make dowel center marks that match exactly.

—Bernard Paumier, Baltimore, Ohio

How to prevent twisted frames

Having the frame of a cabinet door turn out twisted after gluing can be a real disappointment, to say the least.

TIP: Before gluing and clamping, dry-fit the frame members together and lay a straightedge across adjoining members to make sure all surfaces are in the same plane. If they aren't, make sure your cuts are square and splines are the same thickness. Add a perpendicular clamp if necessary, then recheck with the straightedge before gluing.

—From the WOOD magazine shop

Mini-lathe for oversize dowels

Stock wood-dowel diameters are often slightly too large for the holes that you've drilled.

TIP: To assure a snug fit—and avoid the possibility of splitting your workpiece—chuck the dowel into a drill press or portable drill and sand the piece as it spins. To maintain a consistent diameter (and keep your fingers cool), move the sandpaper up and down the dowel as you sand. Don't oversand!

—From the WOOD magazine shop

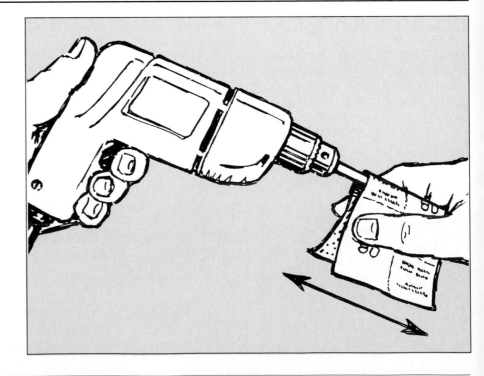

Layout and Measuring

Two ways to measure diameters

Accurately measuring the diameter of an object smaller than 1" can be difficult if you don't have a calipers. Likewise, it's tough to determine the exact diameter of larger round objects.

TIP I: Use squarely cut wood strips and a ruler to determine the diameter of small objects, such as bolts or toy parts. Butt the two strips against the item you're measuring, and align one end with a mark on the scale as shown *below* to take your reading. That's it!

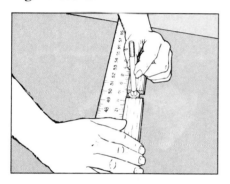

TIP 2: On larger objects, use two framing squares or a framing square and a combination square as shown *below* to determine the object's diameter. To ensure accuracy, set the tools aside and measure the item a second time.

—Denis Marchand, Sherbrooke, Quebec

A tip from the sewing basket

Carbon paper becomes hard to use when transferring paper patterns to dark woods such as walnut. The dark lines are barely visible, and don't erase easily.

TIP: White carbon paper, found in many art and crafts shops, is ideal for transferring patterns to dark wood or hardboard. And, you can remove the pattern lines with a pencil eraser. One manufacturer, Saral® Paper Co., 322 W. 57th St., Suite 30-T, New York, NY 10019, markets their product under the name "Saral® Transfer Paper."

—Cobert LeMunyan, Troutman, N.C.

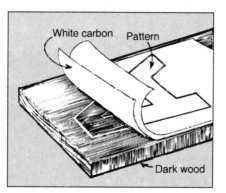

White carbon Pattern

Dark wood

An eraser you'll almost never wear down

You should always be careful to erase pencil marks before sanding wood projects, but laying your hands on a pencil with an eraser that's not worn out isn't always easy to do.

TIP: The cleaning stick that does such a fantastic job of cleaning your abrasive belts makes just about the finest pencil eraser you'll ever find. Use it for eliminating light marks when a standard eraser can't be found. It's tough, economical, and sure to last a long time.

—William Becker, Deep River, Conn.

Finger marking gauge

You won't have to search for a straightedge with this always-at-hand technique.

TIP: Here's an easy trick for marking rough layouts or dividing boards into approximate cuts. Cradle a pencil between your thumb and index fingers, resting it against the middle finger. By sliding the tip of your middle finger along a board's edge, you'll mark a parallel line. Adjust your middle finger's position on the pencil to control distance from the edge. Watch out for splinters.

—From the *WOOD* magazine shop

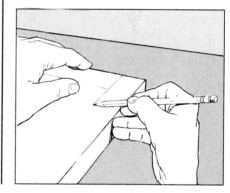

Abrasive belt cleaner

Layout and Measuring

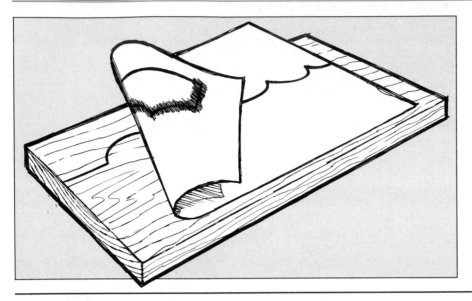

An alternative way to trace a pattern

Carbon paper can be hard to come by when you need it. Also, it's often awkward to use.

TIP: With a No. 2 or softer lead pencil, copy your own pattern without carbon paper. On the back side of the pattern, rub the pencil over *only* the portions you will transfer. Now, position the pattern and trace it as you normally do. If the pattern is one that you will frequently transfer, you can quickly freshen the back side with a pencil.

—Ray Dobelstein, Flemington, N.J.

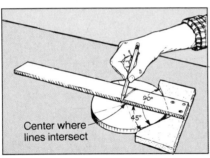

Center where lines intersect

Center issue

It's difficult to locate the center of cylindrical turning stock and other circles with only a straightedge and pencil.

TIP: An inexpensive and simple jig quickly and accurately pinpoints the center of a circle. Cut a 90° notch from ¾" stock. Screw a straightedge over the notched base, as shown, to create a 45° angle. Place the circle against the guide and scribe one line. Rotate the circle about 60° and mark another line. To check the accuracy rotate the circle once more. If the lines form a small triangle, the center is inside the triangle.

—George Harenberg,
Chincoteague, Va.

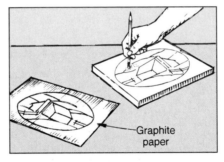

Graphite paper

Here's just the thing for tidy tracings

Using conventional tracing paper to transfer markings for woodburning, carving, or outlining often creates a mess, leaving ugly lines and smears you don't want on the stock.

TIP: Graphite paper makes great stuff for these kinds of tracings. Graphite paper is neat and its marks erase easily, but it's not usually stocked by hardware or office-supply stores. Check hobby shops and stores selling drafting supplies. Saral® is one brand name of graphite paper. (See tip on previous page, *top center,* for address and phone number).

—Sara Jane Treinen, Des Moines

Carbon paper

Super tracing material

Paper and cardboard patterns take a real beating when you trace over them repeatedly. Isn't there a more durable material for use as a pattern?

TIP: Use the original pattern as a master for making a working pattern out of a sheet of matte acetate. This material looks frosty on its matte side, which has a texture that readily takes pencil marks. Use a slightly dull soft-lead pencil to trace the pattern onto the acetate. Now, tape one edge of the acetate sheet to the workpiece, and slip a piece of carbon paper under the pattern, as shown in the drawing *above.* Use a pencil or length of sharpened dowel to trace the image onto the workpiece.

—James R. Gates, Hermitage, Tenn.

Layout and Measuring

Mirror image in half the time

Drawing half of a full-sized pattern is hard enough, but matching the pattern for the other side is just as taxing.

TIP: Draw one-half of your pattern onto a piece of folded paper. Fold and insert a piece of carbon paper, carbon side out, into the folded pattern. Then trace the pattern, open the paper, and unfold a full-sized pattern with identical halves. Now transfer your "perfect" pattern to the workpiece.

—L.E. Masters, Holloman AFB, N.M.

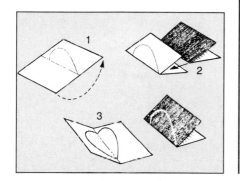

Drawing parallel lines on a cylinder

Sometimes you need to pencil straight, parallel lines along the axis of round stock, such as when you align spindle holes on a dowel rail for a chair back. This can be frustrating without some kind of jig.

TIP: On a flat, smooth work surface, snug together the round stock to be marked and a thin wood strip. Draw the first line on the round stock along the edge where the two pieces meet. (You may need a helper to hold the pieces together while you mark the stock.) Rotate the round stock to draw other parallel lines at the desired spacing, as shown in the drawing *below*.

—From the *WOOD* magazine shop

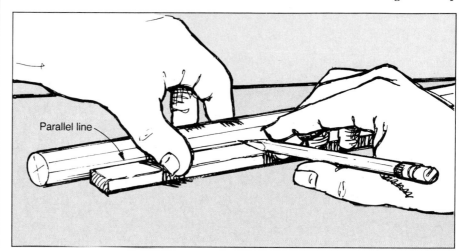

Parallel line

Get double duty from a combination square

Some tasks require using a combination square for measuring and for drawing perpendicular lines, and a marking gauge for drawing lines parallel to an edge on a long work surface. Wouldn't it be nice if one tool could do both jobs?

TIP: Drill a 1/16″ hole through the center of the guide slot in the blade at the 1″ mark as shown. Insert a pencil tip or a scribe through the hole for marking. To figure the distance from the mark to the edge of the stock, remember to subtract 1″ from the distance shown on the scale where it intersects the crosspiece. Hold the pencil and square steady as you mark.

—R.L. Watkins, Naches, Wash.

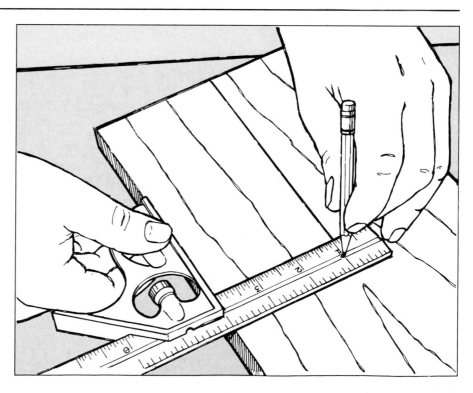

Layout and Measuring

Place photocopied pattern face down

Iron out your pattern problems

Full-sized patterns, such as the ones often found in WOOD *magazine, greatly simplify transferring those patterns to workpieces. However, you still need to either trace the pattern onto the wood surface using carbon paper, graphite paper, or similar products, or adhere the pattern with spray adhesive. You can simplify this process even further with a photocopier.*

TIP: Photocopy the pattern, lay the copy facedown on the workpiece, and transfer the pattern with a clothes iron. Set the iron to the low setting (no steam), and run the iron over the pattern. Then, slowly peel up sections of the copy to make sure all the lines transferred. If not, just go over them again. Note: the pattern will be reversed, so this procedure won't work for all designs.

—M.B. Coyner, Solvang, Calif.

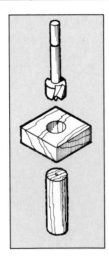

A drill bit finds dead center of a dowel

Locating the center of a wooden dowel can be a hit-or-miss proposition if you try to do it with a straightedge and a pencil. Typically, the smaller the dowel, the greater the chance for missing the middle.

TIP: Hit the center by using a Forstner bit of the same diameter as the dowel to bore a hole through a block of scrapwood. Then, insert the dowel into the hole on one side of the block and the bit on the other side. Press in slightly as you twist the bit a few times to mark the center of the dowel.

—From the *WOOD* magazine shop

A way to leave your mark

How can you draw a line parallel to the edge of a board when your marking gauge, try square, or combination square isn't handy (or long enough)?

TIP: Use your tape measure. First, measure the desired width and lock the tape in place. Then, using the tape body as an edge guide, hold a pencil against the hook, as shown. Slide the tape along steadily as you mark.

—From the **WOOD magazine shop**

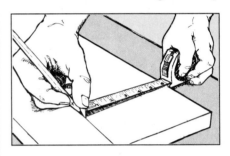

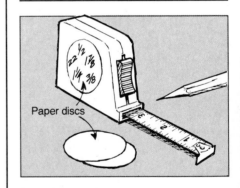

Paper discs

Noteworthy idea for shop scribblers

All too often, there's not a scrap of paper within reach to jot down figures and calculations.

TIP: You'll always have paper as near as your tape measure if you rubber-cement a piece to your tape-measure case. You can write and erase many sets of figures before replacing the paper. Those yellow self-adhesive notes also work well.

—Steve Tegtmeier, Pittsburgh

Layout and Measuring

Turn a yardstick into a large-circle compass

Attempting to draw large circles perfectly with a length of string can transform the coolest worker into a muttering grump.

TIP: For a trusty compass that makes it easy to draw circles of many sizes, drill 5/64" holes at every 1/8" mark in the first inch of a metal yardstick. Now, drill 5/64" holes at every inch on the rest of the yardstick's length. This also works fine in a wooden yardstick. Just space the holes 1/4" apart in the first inch for strength.

To draw a circle with a 27¾" radius, for example, tap a 19- or 20-gauge brad through the drilled hole at the 1/4" mark. Next, insert a pencil point into the 28" hole (28" – 1/4" = 27¾") and draw your circle.

—Walter S. Thomas, Jr., Drexel Hill, Pa.

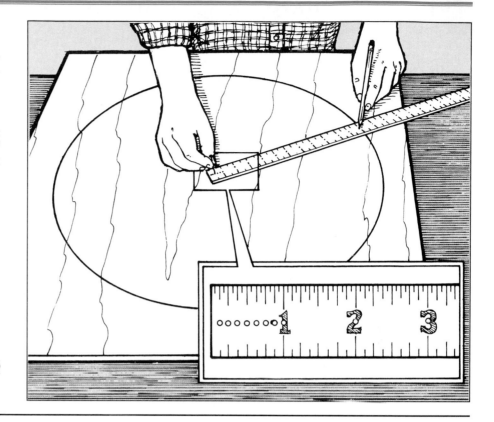

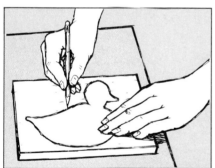

Tough-guy templates

What's a good material for making large, durable templates or patterns for repeating cutouts in plywood or other materials?

TIP: Make your templates out of scraps of plastic laminate, such as that used for countertops. Tape your pattern to the laminate and cut out the shape on a scrollsaw fitted with a fine-tooth blade. The laminate is durable, yet easy to cut and file to precise shapes. Also, you can pencil notes on it and later erase the pencil marks.

—Chip Schmidt, Cedar Falls, Iowa

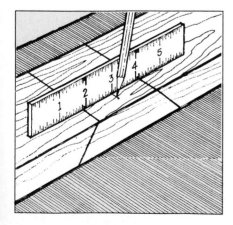

Fast and accurate way to find center

Locating the center between two points often involves a lot of guesswork or math.

TIP: Here's a way to mark a center quickly and accurately. As shown at *left*, just set a rule between the two points so two different inch marks fall equal distances from the two points. The inch mark that falls halfway between the points indicates the center. In this example, we've positioned the 2" and 4" marks 1/8" inside the two points. The center falls at the 3" mark.

—From the *WOOD* magazine shop

Layout and Measuring

Fast method of rescaling plans
Reducing or enlarging patterns usually means spending hours at the drawing board to replot the pattern on graph paper.

TIP: Photocopy several increased and decreased copies of a 12″ ruler, scaled at various ratios such as 25, 50, 75, 125, 150 and 175 percent. Glue the photocopies to pieces of wood as shown at *right*. Then, use the full-sized ruler to measure the original object or pattern. Next, determine the increase or decrease in size needed. For example, we measured the original 10½″-high candlestick shown at *near right*, and laid out a larger-proportioned candlestick using the 175 percent ruler to create an 18⅜″-high candlestick.

—**Kenneth A. Storey, Chattanooga, Tenn.**

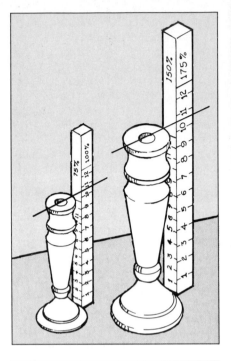

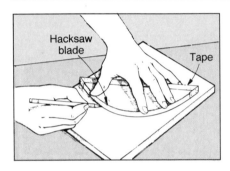

A hacksaw blade can help you draw curves
Occasionally you have to draw a curved line but have no template or guide to create a smooth, pleasing arc. You can buy such templates at art-supply stores, but at a premium price.

TIP: Make an instant template by bowing a hacksaw blade to the curvature you need and holding it in place with a length of masking tape. As a guide for drawing larger or more complicated curves, use a bandsaw blade and hold it in place with brads if necessary.

—**Marvin O. Gennrich, Austin, Minn.**

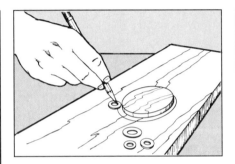

Roll along easily with template enlargements
Enlarging templates by small increments—such as ¼″ or ½″—can be a pain, especially when you're trying to increase the dimensions of a curved or irregularly shaped object. Sometimes, you need to draw template offset lines that match a router guide bushing. Here's a solution utilizing parts on hand.

TIP: Use a flat metal washer as a spacer between the edge of the template and the point of your pencil as illustrated *above*. Washers come in many different sizes, giving you a wide choice in enlarging capabilities. Maintain steady pressure on the pencil as you draw.

—**From the *WOOD* magazine shop**

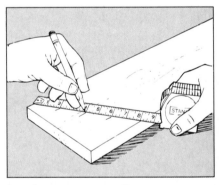

Laying out equal parts
Ever wondered how to quickly divide and mark a board into equal parts without lots of mathematical calculations?

TIP: Lay a measuring tape or rule diagonally across the stock. Then, adjust the angle until the near edge of the board aligns with an inch designation that's divisible by the number of parts you want. The example shown divides the board into four. If you want three parts, you'd place the 9 on the board's edge.

—**From the *WOOD* magazine shop**

Money Savers

Duct tape extends the life of sandpaper

Sandpaper quickly wears out when you smooth curved surfaces.

TIP: Fortify your sandpaper with duct tape as a backing when sanding chair rungs, spindles, and other abrasive-beating surfaces. You may need to use tin snips to cut the reinforced sandpaper.

—Dr. Donald A. Keiser, Saginaw, Mich.

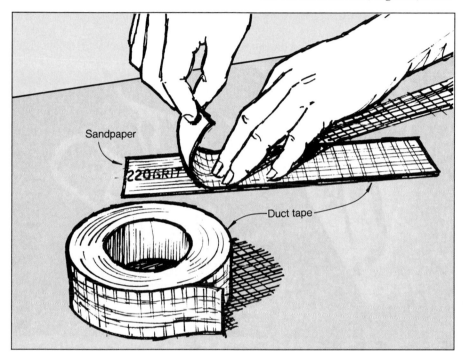

Sandpaper

Duct tape

Give your throwaway paintbrushes a second life

It seems a shame to throw out any part of those disposable foam brushes, even though they are relatively inexpensive.

TIP: Get more than your money's worth from those brushes by recycling the handles for such uses as paddles for spreading glue and stirring such materials as putty and epoxy glue. Strip off the foam and reshape the handles on a belt sander if necessary for the task you decide to give it.

—Ken Thompson, Sheridan, Ill.

Remove used foam

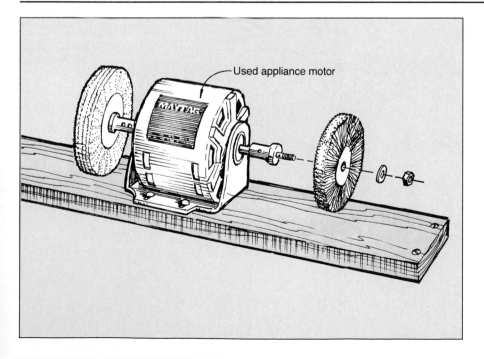

Used appliance motor

Low-cost grinder

The cost of a new grinder keeps many woodworkers from purchasing this practical tool.

TIP: Save a few dollars and pick up a used washer or dryer motor from an appliance repair service or salvage yard. (Try to find a motor with two shafts.) Mount the motor to a stand or a wood base, add an electrical switch, and attach a work arbor (available at hardware stores) to each shaft. You can reverse the wiring on most motors to create your own grinder or buffer.

—Harley Refsal, Decorah, Iowa

Money Savers

Recycling paint thinner

It seems a waste (ecologically and monetarily) to discard paint thinner after using it only once for cleaning brushes.

TIP: Recycle that thinner for additional cleanup jobs by storing it in a coffee can with a sealable lid. In a few days, the solids settle out, so you can pour most of the reusable thinner off the top and discard the remaining goo.

—Jack Mitchell, Concordia, Kan.

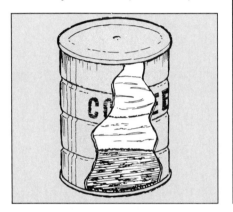

3-for-1 paint roller

If you use 3″ paint rollers, here's how to save a few bucks:

TIP: Make your own 3″ rollers. With a hacksaw or other fine-toothed saw, cut a 9″ roller into three equal parts. Recently, we needed 3″ rollers, which cost $1.59 each. The 9″ version sold for $1.90 each. For each 9″ roller we bought, we came out $2.87 ahead.

—From the *WOOD* magazine shop

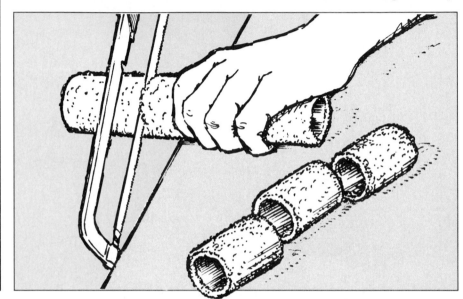

Sharp way to economize

No matter how long the jigsaw blade is, just a few of the teeth are doing the cutting for most operations. Those teeth quickly become dull.

TIP: Add an auxiliary plate to the bottom of your jigsaw to extend the life of its blades. The thickness of the plate will depend on the material being cut, but the plate needs to be at least as thick as the length of the saw stroke. As a bonus, the auxiliary plate won't allow the blade to wander as much. Use wide double-sided adhesive tape to mount the plate.

—R.T. Dunnington, Centerville, Ohio

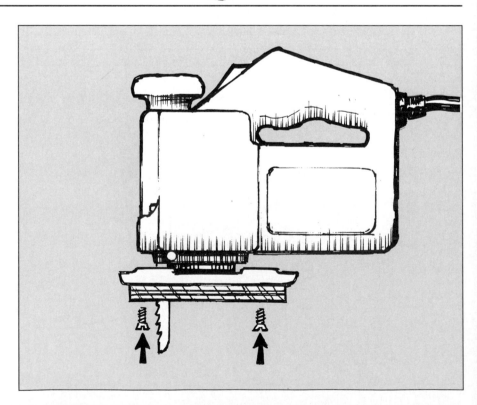

Organizing Your Shop

A swinging way to save bench space

If you have a small, cramped shop, you probably value every extra inch of bench space you can get. Bench-mounted grinders and similar bench-mounted tools can really chew up the space in a hurry.

TIP: To better use limited bench space, you can install your grinder so it swings down underneath the bench when you're through using it. To do this, screw a pair of 6" or larger strap hinges to the underside of the bench, as shown in the illustrations *below*. Hammer the ends back to lie flat on the bench top. Next, attach a plywood base to the hinges, then bolt the tool onto the base. (Countersink the bolts so the base will sit flush on the bench.) Finally, install a pair of screw eyes and a wire hook (a coat hanger works well) to hold the tool back away from your knees in its storage position.

—Fred Easley, Jerseyville, Ill.

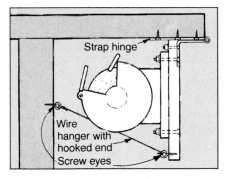

Strap hinge

Wire hanger with hooked end
Screw eyes

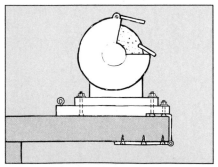

Vinegar takes sticky epoxy off your fingers

Even the most persnickety of woodworkers rarely avoid an oops with freshly mixed epoxy glue. Accidental drips and smears quickly show up on the materials being glued and on the worker's hands. Trying to wipe up these little messes before the epoxy sets often falls short of the success you'd like.

TIP: Dampen a clean cloth with white vinegar (available in grocery stores) that contains 5 percent acetic acid. Then, quickly wipe up the epoxy before it has a chance to set.

—Walt Easley, Gladbrook, Iowa

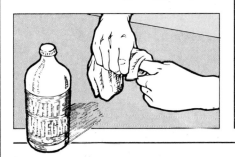

"Nutty" idea for plugging caulking tubes

Each time you grab a partially used tube of caulk or adhesive, the contents have solidified to brick hardness in the nozzle.

TIP: Large electrical wire nuts with soft "skirts" are ideal for temporarily sealing caulk and adhesive tubes. Avoid using hard plastic wire nuts that may weaken in the solvents used to make adhesive. Blue or gray wire nuts made by the 3M company are suitable.

—Ron Steelman, St. Paul, Minn.

Electrical wire nut

Two safe saw-blade holders

Circular saw blades—sharp or dull—need tender, loving care. These two blade holders will protect the blades—and your hands.

TIP: Make a blade holder like the one shown *below, left* to cart your dull blades to the sharpening shop. When you get the sharp blades back from the shop, store them in a wall-mounted rack like the one shown *below, right.*

—George Gildea, Fort Thomas, Ky.

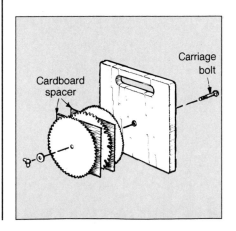

Cardboard spacer

Carriage bolt

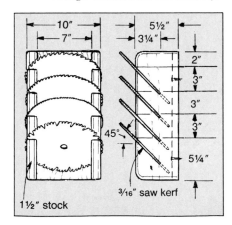

10"
7"
5½"
3¼"
2"
3"
3"
3"
45°
5¼"
³⁄₁₆" saw kerf
1½" stock

Organizing Your Shop

The search is over

Coffee cans and various jars are ideal for storing nails, screws, and other hardware—but it still takes lots of time to sort through the container contents.

TIP: Cut a large hole from the side of a 1-gallon plastic milk or bleach bottle. Pour the contents of the container through the opening. Use the bottle's spout as a funnel to return the hardware to the proper container. (The milk jugs can transport small tools, too.)

—Rev. Daniel Presswood, Medora, Ill.

Cut out

Low and inside planer

Many woodworkers don't have extra work surface to keep a thickness planer set up. The solution may be right at your feet.

TIP: The space you need for a thickness planer may be located beneath your workbench. There is plenty of room under many workbenches for compact planers, such as the Ryobi AP-10.

—Larry Naumann, St. Louis,

Thickness planer

Protection plan for WOOD magazine

Even when you try to be careful, the woodworking plans in WOOD magazine can take a real beating from liquid spills in your shop. And, how many times have you employed an awkward weight to hold the magazine open to a certain place, only to tear a page when you reposition the magazine? Before you know it, you've accidentally soiled or torn your only copy of WOOD magazine.

TIP: Preserve the entire magazine with a protective holder like the one shown *below.* Start with a base of ½" plywood large enough to hold *WOOD* magazine (18×13"), glue a ½ × ½" lip along one side of the longer edges, fit an 18×12½" sheet of ⅛" acrylic, and install ³⁄₁₆" stove bolts with wing nuts to hold it all together. Bolts should protrude about ¾" through the base. For quicker page changes, you can install hinges along one side in place of two of the wing nuts.

—Julie Manuel, Oklahoma City, Okla.

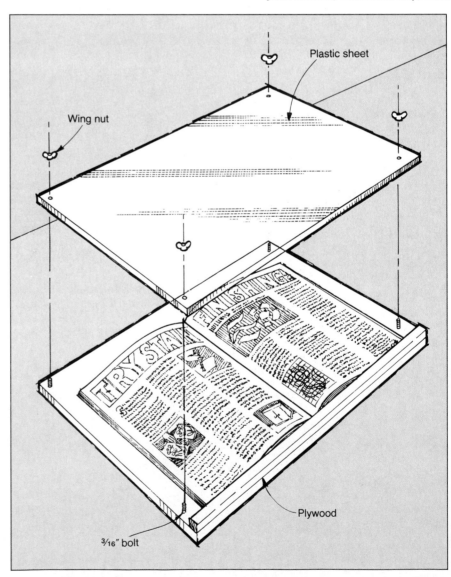

Plastic sheet

Wing nut

Plywood

³⁄₁₆" bolt

Organizing Your Shop

Another good use for magnets

Many stationary power tools have removable locking switches or keys. Unfortunately, most of them won't attach to your key ring.

TIP: Epoxy a round hobby magnet to the switch or key and attach it to an inconspicuous metal part of the tool where it won't be lost.

—William M. Resnik, Albuquerque, N.M.

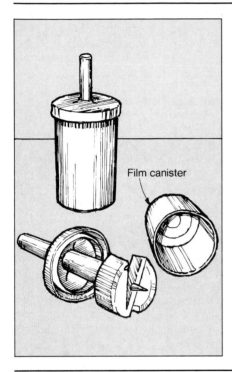

Film canister

Picture-perfect storage for Forstner bits

Forstner bits cost too much to leave them loose and unprotected in toolboxes. Yet you can't store them the way you can other drill bits because their shape is too awkward.

TIP: Plastic 35mm film canisters make handy and durable protectors for Forstner bits up to 1⅛" in diameter. (They're free, too.) Slip the shaft through a hole cut in the canister lid and store as shown at *left*. In addition, the lid makes a good depth gauge. Use masking tape on the canister to identify the bit diameter. You can protect router and specialty bits with the same technique and materials.

—Eddie Tomlinson, Alcolu, S.C.

A new wrinkle on making storage bins

Most every woodworker accumulates an assortment of fasteners and small parts that requires systematic storage. Otherwise, clutter and chaos soon take over.

TIP: You can easily make storage bins of one-gallon cans used for packaging liquids such as paint thinner. Dave Wilson of Aberdeen, Wash., sent in a shop tip describing one style (shown *below, at top*). Cutting away the corner diagonally renders a container of a different breed. Use tin snips to do the shearing and turn over the sharp edges with a pair of pliers and a hammer. The second style creates a container you can pick up by the handle and carry without spillage.

—Clarence R. Evans, Cape May Court House, N.J.

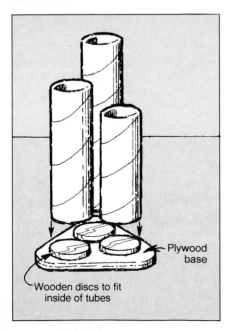

Plywood base

Wooden discs to fit inside of tubes

All-round dowel storage

Dowels and threaded rods never seem to stay put in their assigned storage nooks. The wooden dowels are apt to warp or break before they are used.

TIP: Cardboard cores from carpet rolls, make excellent storage tubes for round material such as dowels. You can obtain the tubes from a local carpet dealer, then cut the tubes to various lengths (try 12", 20", and 30" for starters). Glue and nail wooden discs to a plywood base and then fit the tubes over the disks. The cardboard tubes also can be used between ceiling joists to store the same types of materials.

—From the *WOOD* magazine shop

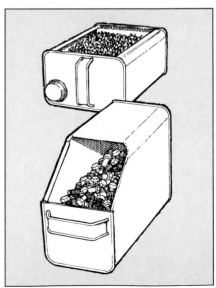

Organizing Your Shop

Keeping blades in apple-pie order

Tablesaw blades pose fascinating dangers to curious children exploring in the workshop.

TIP: Plastic containers for keeping and transporting pies safely store saw blades, too. Separate the blades with cardboard spacers. The lids form a tight seal on the 12″ containers; they also seal out moisture.

—Shauna Beintema, San Diego

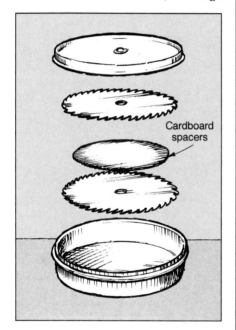

Cardboard spacers

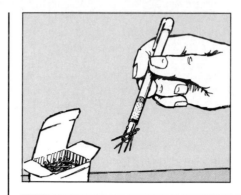

Quick picker-upper

It's just about impossible to pick up all the brads after you've spilled the box.

TIP: To avoid those frustrating spills, insert a small magnet into the box and grab brads, tacks, or small nails a few at a time. Some magnets are shaped like a pencil and clip onto your shirt pocket.

—From the *WOOD* magazine shop

Put that chuck key where you'll always find it

A drill press chuck key has a way of disappearing when you want it. Many times, it's hidden out of sight in some corner of your shop. You can waste a lot of time looking for it.

TIP: Use cloth-backed, double-sided carpet tape to attach a small magnet in a convenient location on the head of your drill press. The magnet will hold that elusive chuck key and keep it from wandering.

—Lyle Kruger, Effingham, Ill.

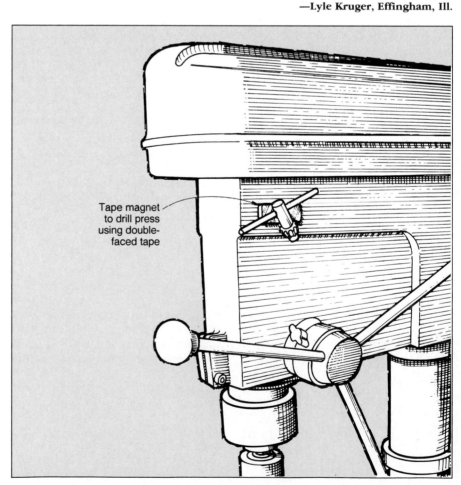

Tape magnet to drill press using double-faced tape

Organizing Your Shop

This tip is on the level

In a garage or crowded workshop, it's time-consuming to reposition stationary tools on a level spot.

TIP: Once you've found that perfect level spot, spray-paint around each leg to mark the spot for repositioning the machine.

—Frank Zalenski, Vancouver, Wash.

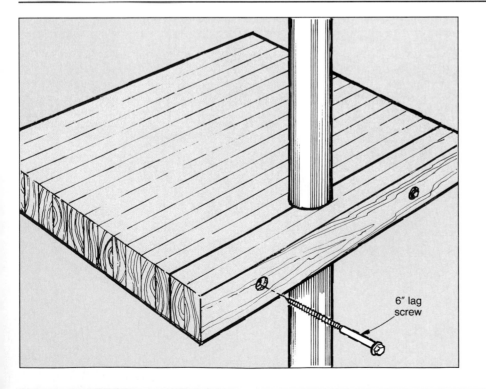

6" lag screw

Power tool holsters

In a confined work space, everything ends up in a pile along the back edge of the workbench.

TIP: Use thin-wall plastic pipe to custom-make holders for power and hand tools. Cut the pipe into 8" lengths, and notch to fit various tools. Drill a hole in the back side and attach the holder to a wall with screws.

—Steve E. Miller, Dallas, Ore.

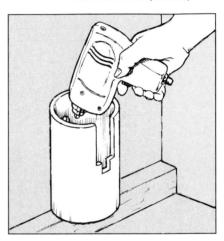

Outstanding in a supporting role

If you have a basement shop, there's a good chance you've occasionally cursed the steel posts that support beams in many newer homes.

TIP: Put those posts to work in your workshop as a stand for a grinder or drill press. Determine the size of the stand your tool requires, and glue a stack of 2×4s together as shown at *left*. Now, lay out and cut a hole the diameter of the post less $1/16$" toward the rear of the table. Rip the lamination through the hole. Then "clamp" the two parts of the table around the posts with 6" lag screws.

—Gary Paine, Davison, Mich.

Organizing Your Shop

Vise magnetism

Screws, bolts, nuts, and other small parts just sort of seem to wander away when you work around a vise.

TIP: Epoxy a small magnet to the side of your vise to keep closer tabs on your footloose hardware. This handy addition to your workshop will save a lot of time looking for metal parts that disappear all too quickly.

—**Randy Marras, Chicago**

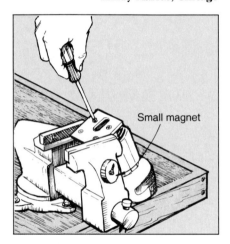

Small magnet

Containers for powdered abrasives

Abrasives such as pumice and rottenstone create a gritty mess when applied. It's also hard to find just the right applicator for rubbing out a finish with these materials.

TIP: An old pair of salt and pepper shakers make good storage containers. Just shake the abrasive onto the surface to be worked. Use a felt chalkboard eraser or piece of dense foam to rub out the finish.

—**From the *WOOD* magazine shop**

PUMICE

Handy tape dispenser

In many shops, finding the right tape at the right time can be a problem. Once located, it's often covered with sawdust, wood shavings, and other debris.

TIP: To keep various types and sizes of tape in one handy location, use scrapwood and a piece of dowel or broomstick to make a tape dispenser. An old hacksaw blade reinforced with a wooden strip makes an excellent cutting edge.

—**Dwight Blakeney, Seaford, Del.**

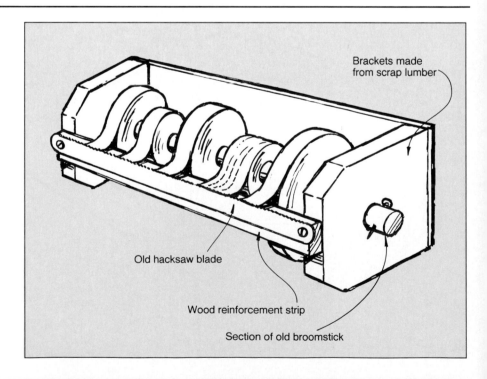

Brackets made from scrap lumber

Old hacksaw blade

Wood reinforcement strip

Section of old broomstick

Radial-Arm Saw Strategies

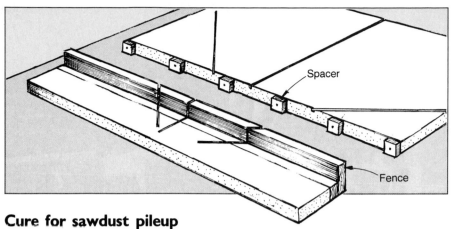

Cure for sawdust pileup

Sawdust accumulating near your saw fence causes inaccurate cuts.

TIP: From a scrap of ¼" birch plywood, cut several spacers 1" long and to a width ¹/₁₆" less than the thickness of the front table. Attach the spacers to the back edge of the front table with flathead wood screws, aligning the spacer bottoms with the bottom edge of the table. This leaves the spacers recessed ¹/₁₆" below the table surface. Space these 12" apart. Make sure the screwheads are flush with the face of the spacers. Install the fence and back table. Readjust the rip scales on the saw to compensate for the extra ¼" space between the fence and table. Sawdust will fall through the gaps.

—Bill Pearce, Jacksonville, Fla.

Escape route for cut-off pieces

A possible hazard when making miter cuts with a radial-arm saw occurs when cut-off pieces become trapped between the blade and the fence. The spinning blade can launch these scraps like bullets.

TIP: Notch out about 1½" of the fence as shown. This prevents the cut-off scrap from becoming a projectile by binding between the blade and fence.

—From the *WOOD* magazine shop

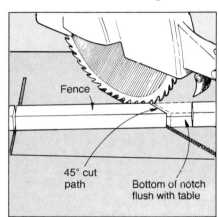

Quick help for accurate cuts

Measuring and marking get real old in a hurry when cutting parts for a project that requires several duplicate pieces. And, it's nearly impossible to cut pieces of exactly identical lengths using a tape measure.

TIP: When you install a new fence on your radial-arm saw, draw marks at ¼" intervals on both sides of the blade. Or, buy an adhesive-backed rule. Then, you'll always have a ruler to help you instantly measure stock on the table.

To get those exact repetitive cuts, build a clamplike adjustable stop by cutting pieces of scrap as shown *inset*. The middle piece should be slightly thinner than the thickness of the fence. Quarter-inch dowels keep the pieces aligned. To avoid sawdust buildup, the stop should ride on the fence and not touch the table.

—Gary R. Kenyon, Oak Creek, Wis.

Radial-Arm Saw Strategies

Rolls-Royce stop block

Stop blocks come in real handy when you want to cut several pieces to the same length. But you usually have to move the block to ensure that both ends are squared.

TIP: With the gate closed, position and clamp the block to the fence so that it's the exact finished length of the pieces away from the blade. Open the gate, position the workpiece, and cut. Then close the gate, flip the workpiece end for end, and make a final cut. The movable, hinged end gate of this stop block works on either side of a radial-arm or tablesaw blade.

—From the *WOOD* magazine shop

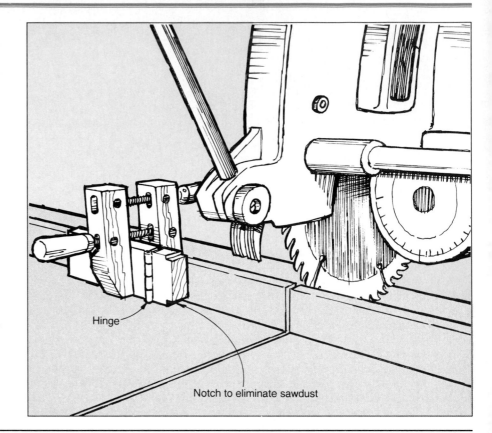

Hinge

Notch to eliminate sawdust

Borrowed from the family sewing kit

Ripping various widths of material on a radial-arm saw requires a lot of setup time. How can you speed things up?

TIP: With the radial-arm blade set for ripping, turn on the saw, lower the blade, and cut a 1/16"-deep groove in the tabletop. Then pull the blade slowly toward and then away from you to create a dished-out groove.

Glue a paper or cloth tape measure to the bottom of the groove. When you're ready to rip, set the blade so that it just clears the scale. Now you don't need to raise and lower the blade each time you set up to rip a different width of material.

—Fred Schwend, Mira Loma, Calif.

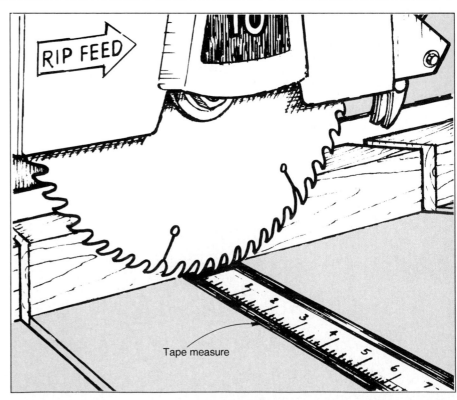

RIP FEED

Tape measure

Routing

When you don't know which way to turn

If you're like us, you may have a devil of a time remembering whether to turn the wrench clockwise or counterclockwise to loosen or tighten the collet that holds router bits.

TIP: Label the tightening direction on the router body with a permanent marker so you'll make the right move every time.

—From the *WOOD* magazine shop

Router flush trimmer

Particularly with today's thin veneers, it's tough to sand flush an edge band without sanding through the veneer.

TIP: This simple jig does the trick. Remove the plastic router base and screw on a piece of ¼" hardboard as shown. Adjust a ½" straight router bit flush with the bottom of the hardboard. Keep the router absolutely vertical and it will cut away any material not flush with the jig.

—From the *WOOD* magazine shop

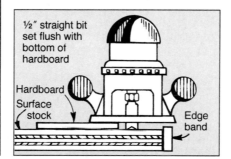

½" straight bit set flush with bottom of hardboard

Hardboard

Surface stock

Edge band

Stop block with an angle

Many woodworkers clamp a square block of wood to their saw or router table to serve as a stop for making repeated cuts. But the accumulation of sawdust and chips against the block results in inconsistent lengths.

TIP: Turn the block so that only a corner of it stops the movement of your workpieces. Sawdust will now blow to the side and back of the block, leaving the front clear to stop the cut.

—Richard Kandus, Arcata, Calif.

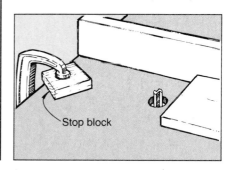

Stop block

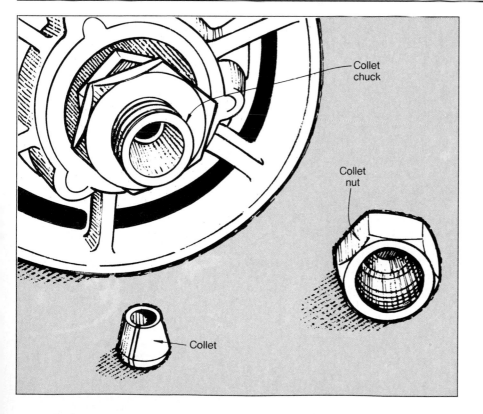

Collet chuck

Collet nut

Collet

Steel wool whisks grime from the router collet

When fine wood dust and other residue collect inside the collet assembly on a router, you'll have to struggle to change bits.

TIP: Use a small wad of fine steel wool to scour out the gummy accumulation. This effectively removes the grime without marring or scratching the smooth metal surfaces.

—From the *WOOD* magazine shop

Routing

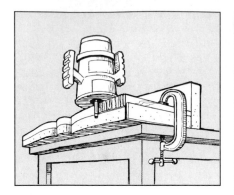

Work-saving router template for curved pieces

In production work, when many pieces of the same shape have to be cut and routed, you need something to help increase speed and accuracy.

TIP: Build a plywood template for your router. Make a full-sized layout of the finished piece in plywood. Add cleats to the back and sides where no routing will be done. Also glue strips of sandpaper to the top corners of the template so the work won't vibrate around.

Rough-cut the workpiece to within $1/32''$ of the line, then clamp it to the template. Using a router with a flush-trimming carbide bit and ball-bearing guide, trim off excess as shown.

—From the *WOOD* magazine shop

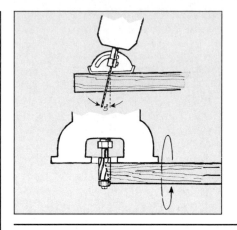

Trueing curved cuts

Curved cuts made with a jigsaw are rarely top-to-bottom square.

TIP: Use both a jigsaw and router for a true edge. Make the cutout with the jigsaw blade set at an angle away from the piece. Turn the board over and rout away excess with a carbide straight cutter bit. Set the bearing guide to protrude halfway below the board.

—From the *WOOD* magazine shop

Two tips for plunging to precise depths

Plunge routers excel in certain operations, such as making signs, cutting dadoes and rabbets, making hanger holes in the back of plaques, and molding edges. Many of these jobs require precise cutting depths.

TIP 1: To fine-adjust plunge routers with thread-rod length adjustments for exact depth of cut, plunge the bit slightly deeper (about $1/16''$) than desired and lock into place. Bring down the upper nut on the rod until it comes into contact with the router housing. Now, release the lock and slowly loosen the nut, allowing the router's spring action to lift the bit to the precise depth as shown in the drawing at *right*. Tighten the nut to prevent any vertical movement.

—From the *WOOD* magazine shop

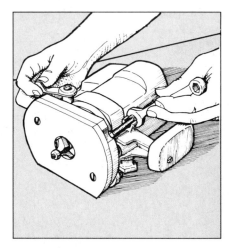

TIP 2: Using the depth gauges on plunge routers often creates an irritating variance in rabbet and dado cuts. Try this remedy: Cut a set of precision shims or gauges made of hardwood, aluminum, brass, or plastic in common thicknesses such as $1/8''$, $1/4''$, $3/8''$, and so on. A convenient size is $3/4 \times 3''$. Drill a $1/4''$ hole in one end for hanging and label each block according to its thickness. Use these to preset your router depth consistently as shown in the drawing at *right*.

—Eugene Fischer, Houston

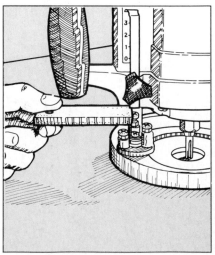

At-a-glance profile of router bits

Because the profile of a router bit appears to be the opposite shape of the cut it makes, it often takes a second glance to select the correct cutter for the desired shape.

TIP: For a reference of the bit profile, shape an 8″ length of scrap material with each bit. Trim the profile to a shorter length and hang the profile near the respective bit. Hold the profile to the end of your workpiece before you make any cuts. Be careful to always replace the profiles and bits in the correct storage spots.

—From the *WOOD* magazine shop

Handy gauge for router-fence setting

The bit clearance cutouts in some router fences make it difficult to use a rule to determine accurate bit-to-fence spacing.

TIP: A 3×6″ piece of ½″ plywood makes a good base for a gauge. Cut a 45° bevel on one end of the stock and glue or tack a section of tape measure to the gauge as shown *below*. Held perpendicularly to the fence, this gauge assures accurate measuring. Held vertically, it reads elevation of the bit. This gauge also comes in handy for setting the rip fence on a tablesaw.

—Eben H. Gustafson,
Martinsburg, W. Va.

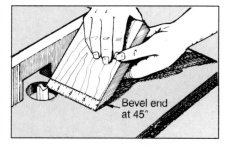

Bevel end at 45°

Help for removing stubborn router bits

Sometimes a burred bit shaft or pinched collet makes it difficult to remove a bit from your router. Attempting to force such a bit loose can result in damaging it or the router itself.

TIP: Leave about ⅛″ of clearance on the shaft in the collet when you install the bit. This gives you room to insert the tips of a needle-nose pliers, which will act as a lever when you back off the collet nut. Be careful not to damage the cutting edges, especially with carbide-tipped bits.

—Buddy Munro, Little Neck, N.Y.

Safety Hints

Here's a "gripping" idea for pushsticks

When working with stationary power tools such as tablesaws, pushsticks make indispensable safety aids. However, unless handled carefully, these stock pushers can slip and cause the very accident they are designed to prevent in the first place.

TIP: To make the pushstick stay put on the workpiece, apply a nonslip coating to the bottom of the stick as illustrated. A 1/16" layer of silicone sealant works nicely. Allow it to dry completely before using.

—Virginia Maples, Old Church, Va.

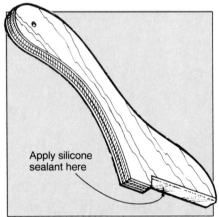

Apply silicone sealant here

Use a comb to hammer your nails—and not your fingers

Anytime you drive small brads and tiny nails, you run the risk of hitting the wrong nail—your fingernail!

TIP: An everyday pocket comb holds those little fasteners.

—Frank A. Erdt, Gum Spring, Va.

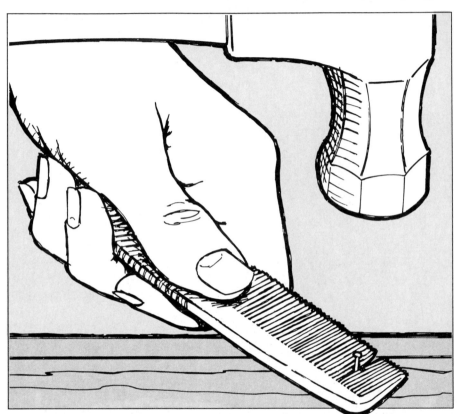

Caution flags for long clamps

Long pipe clamps and bar clamps often stretch well beyond the confines of the stock being held together. In fact, far enough to stick right into the path of some of us who have a knack for bumping and plowing into most anything (make that everything!) that gets in the way. Too often, we pay the price for this shortcoming in scrapes, bruises, and torn clothing.

TIP: Drape brightly colored rags over clamp ends to remind yourself and shop visitors to steer clear of the protrusion.

—From the *WOOD* magazine shop

Safety Hints

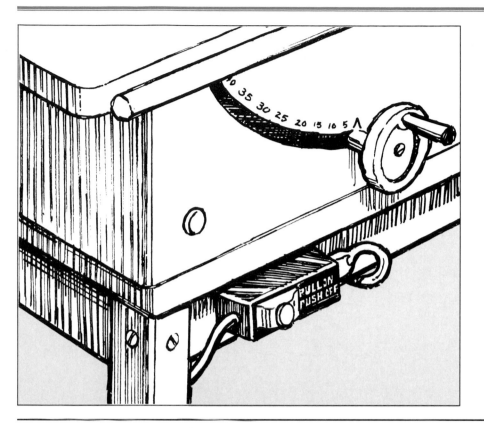

Knee-jerk reaction for tablesaw safety

You're making a cut on your tablesaw when, halfway through, the workpiece goes askew. Yet you can't shut off the saw without taking your hands off the workpiece. This situation can pose a major shop safety problem. What do you do at such times?

TIP: Buy a safety switch that pulls out for the "on" position and pushes in for the "off" position. Mount the switch on the front of your tablesaw at knee height. Now, turning off your saw is as easy as pushing your knee against the switch.

These switches have an added safety feature: Each comes with a plastic key that you can remove to keep little ones from turning on your saw.

—Bruce Wedan, Des Moines

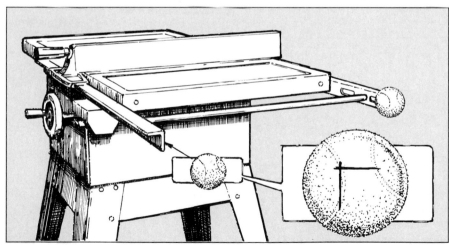

A real "stitch saver"

Some tablesaws have L-shaped metal fence guides protruding at just the right height to inflict painful cuts and bumps on the heads of wee ones. Also at risk are the lower portions of a grown-up's anatomy.

TIP: Cut L-shaped slots in two tennis balls, then slip them over the protruding angles.

—Jerry Swenson, Newport News, Va.

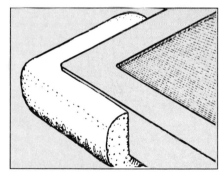

Soften the blow from sharp corners

The corners of the tables on stationary power tools can inflict painful bumps, particularly on the heads of children.

TIP: Cover the sharp metal corners on these machines with lengths of pipe insulation tubing slit open on one side. Glue in place using hotmelt adhesive. Then trim the padding flush with the top of the table.

—Ak Lallas, Viroqua, Wis.

Safety Hints

"Pencil-pusher" safety tip

When miter-cutting, scraps can linger too close to the blade, catch, and kick back.

TIP: The eraser end of a common pencil is a handy way to flick away potential missiles from a tablesaw blade. It's *much* safer than using your fingers to remove wood scraps.

—From the *WOOD* magazine shop

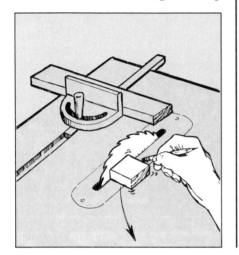

Shock treatment for power cords

When power-cord connectors are subjected to rain or other moisture, the possibility of electrical shock increases.

TIP: Cut a hole in the bottom of a milk jug and pull one cord entirely through the jug, connect, and suspend the connection in the middle of the jug.

—From the *WOOD* magazine shop

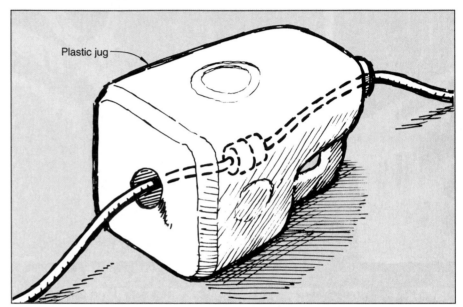

Plastic jug

Klutz-free nailing

No matter how carefully you work, you often end up banging your fingers or the material when driving brads or short finish nails. Drats!

TIP: Start the nail in the thin end of a narrow shim (cedar shingles work well for this). Use the shim to hold the nail in place until you've driven it nearly all the way into the work. Then, pull the shim off the nail and use a nail set to finish the job. No shims available? Use a short length of corrugated cardboard (the backing board of notepads also works well).

—Carl R. Faix, Cherry Hill, N.J.

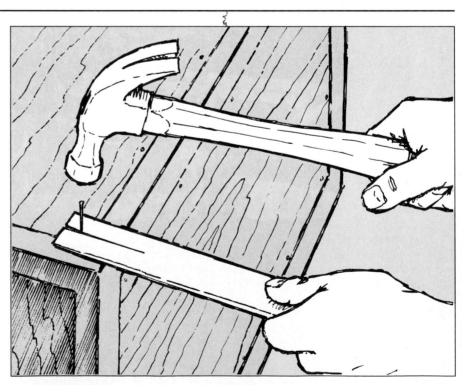

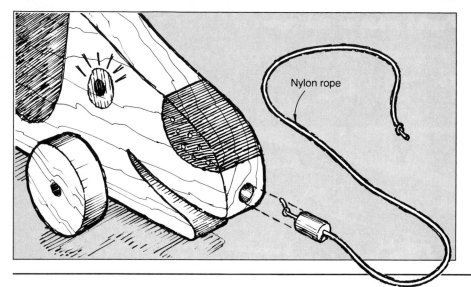

Nylon rope

A knotty solution

It's difficult to avoid screw eyes when a toy needs a pull string. But you worry about tots swallowing such small parts.

TIP: A ½″ dowel and a piece of nylon rope make a good replacement for a screw eye. Drill a ½″ hole about 1″ into the "nose" of the toy. Cut a 1½″ length from a ½″ dowel and drill a ⅛″-diameter hole through the center. Slip a piece of ⅛″ nylon rope through the hole and tie a knot at each end.

—Ron Berlier, Modesto, Calif.

Pin the savage bandsaw

A bandsaw blade can turn vicious and inflict nasty bites, should it jump off the wheels during installation. It's not always easy to keep the blade on one wheel while wrapping it around the other(s).

TIP: Gain a hand to help tame the blade by clipping the blade to one wheel on the saw with two or three clothespins borrowed from the laundry room. This leaves your hands free to slip the blade over the remaining wheel(s).

—David Webber, Chantilly, Va.

Simple chuck key guard

Getting your fingers caught between the teeth of a drill chuck and chuck key (it happens to the best of us!) can add a mighty painful twist to tightening a bit.

TIP: Slipping a washer between those grinding teeth and your fingers neatly solves this problem. Use a partially open vise or a small anvil to support the chuck key, as you gently hammer the handle out of the key (you may need a small punch to remove it completely). Now slip on a large metal washer to act as a shield and tap the handle back in place.

—Louis Mouis, Aurora, Ill.

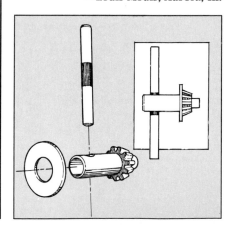

Safety Hints

Hooked on safety

A safety-conscious woodworker always unplugs power tools, but power cords on the floor can be stepped on and damaged.

TIP: Form a hook from electrical wire. Wrap the wire around the cord and hang the cord from some convenient spot on the tool. (P.S.: you'll find that you don't have to crouch down to reach the plug this way, too.)

—**Thomas E. Chaffin, Jr., Mission Viejo, Calif.**

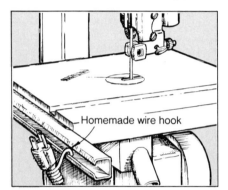

Homemade wire hook

Passing grade on this report

Exposed handsaw blades are a triple threat: They injure careless hands, they inadvertently mar wood, and they damage easily.

TIP: The plastic spines from business-report covers (sold at office-supply stores) perform superbly as blade guards.

—**Carl Dorsch, Oakdale, Pa.**

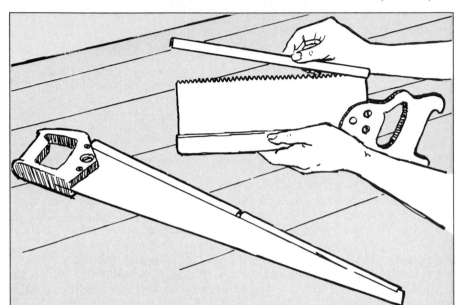

How to outsmart a nail

In a tight spot, it can be impossible to get your fingers around to start a nail or brad.

TIP: A small magnet will hold a brad or nail upright while you tap it into the wood. Note: This tip also helps prevent black and blue fingers, sometimes referred to as "hitting the wrong nail."

—**From the *WOOD* magazine shop**

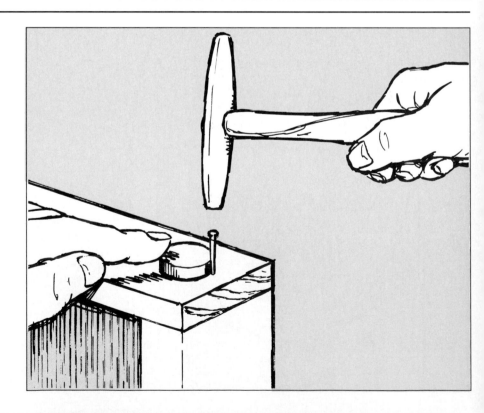

Sanding

A gadget for sanding concave surfaces

Sanding wooden moldings on furniture and other concave surfaces with hand-held sandpaper often results in skinned fingers.

TIP: Gather up an old door hinge, a short length of the appropriate diameter dowel, a piece of sandpaper for the desired grit, and a couple of roundhead machine screws with wing nuts. Cut the dowel to the correct length and the sandpaper to the appropriate dimensions and assemble.

—Fred A. Race, Euclid, Ohio

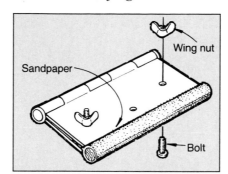

Oversized sanding block

Using a standard-sized sanding block to smooth long, narrow pieces of stock, or panels more than a foot square, produces high or low spots.

TIP: Tape or glue one-half sheet of standard 9×11" sandpaper to a 3×11" block of wood. This oversized block bridges the high and low areas in the material, similar to the effect of a long hand plane.

—From the *WOOD* magazine shop

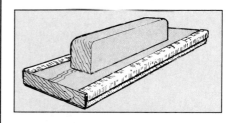

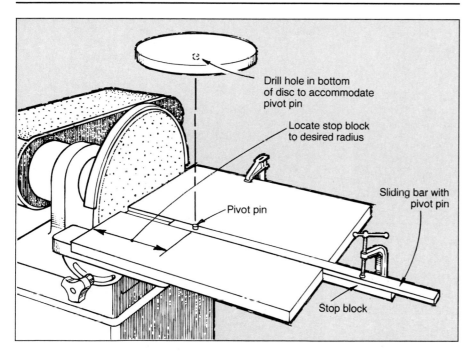

Drill hole in bottom of disc to accommodate pivot pin

Locate stop block to desired radius

Pivot pin

Sliding bar with pivot pin

Stop block

Sand perfect circles

It's practically impossible to cut perfect circles for such projects as wheels or small round tables using a bandsaw or scrollsaw.

TIP: Try a disc sander to achieve true roundness. First, from ¾" plywood, build an auxiliary table (about twice the size of the table on your disc sander) with a ⅜"-deep slot ¾" wide. Now, fit a hardwood bar a few inches longer than the auxiliary table so it slides freely in the slot. About 1" from one end of the slide, fit a ³/₃₂" pin that protrudes ¼" (see drawing *above*). Bore a ³/₃₂" hole at the center of the circular workpiece, place it over the pin on the slide, and slowly advance it into the sanding disc. When you reach the scribed circumference, clamp the slide to the auxiliary table and spin the workpiece for a perfect circle.

—Edward Hanselman, Hoosick Falls, N.Y.

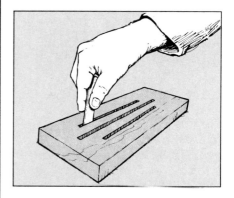

Sanding inside narrow slots

How do you sand the sides of a cut that's, say, only ⅛" wide? Conventional sanding blocks won't work. Sandpaper alone wears down the ends but hardly smooths the middle section.

TIP: An emery board for manicuring fingernails can reach right into those "impossible" places for quick and easy sanding. You also can get the same results by ripping thin wood pieces and gluing or taping sandpaper to them.

—Andrew Dohan, Paoli, Pa.

Sanding

Here's an inexpensive sanding sleeve

It's time consuming to sand the inside of any hole smaller than the diameter of your smallest drum sander.

TIP: Dowels ⅜" or smaller are ideal for sanding difficult surfaces. With a thin-blade saw, slit 2" or 3" into one end of a 5" or 6" dowel. Insert a strip of sandpaper through the slit and wrap the sandpaper tightly counterclockwise around the dowel. Chuck the other end of the dowel and sand.

—Carl Dorsch, Oakdale, Pa.

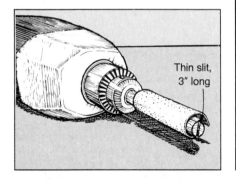

Thin slit, 3" long

Quick sandpaper cutter

How can I divide full sheets of sandpaper into the sizes I use without folding, creasing, and back-creasing, then tearing on a straightedge?

TIP: Fashion a sandpaper ripper with a piece of plywood and an old hacksaw blade. Measure and mark the sizes of paper you normally use on the plywood surface. With wood screws, mount the blade and use thin washers below the blade so the paper can slide under.

—From the *WOOD* magazine shop

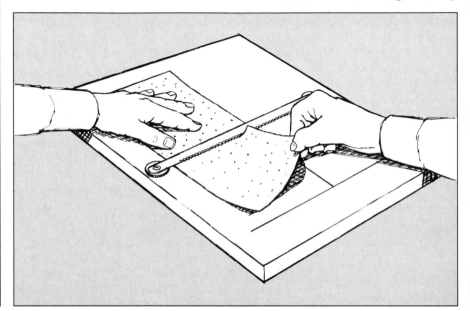

Finger-saving sander for shapely workpieces

Hand-sanding large, contoured shapes, such as lathe turnings and decoys, can wear your fingers to the bone.

TIP: Homemade bow sanders of various sizes give excellent control with less effort. To make one, laminate two pieces of ½" to ¾" plywood together, bandsaw the bow to the desired shape and size, then roundover the edges with a rasp and sandpaper. Then, cut wedge-shaped slots ½" to ¾" deep at each end to accept strips of cloth-backed sanding-belt material. Use the cut-out pieces as wedges to fasten the strips into the slots.

—Lloyd McCabe, Scarborough, Ontario

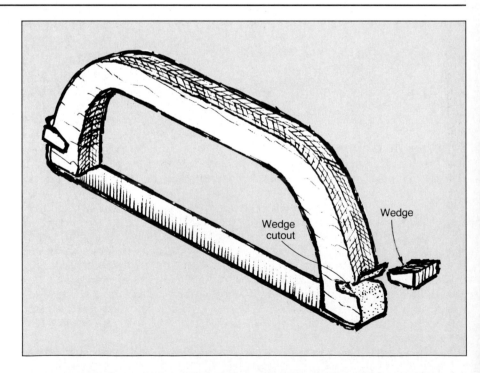

Wedge cutout

Wedge

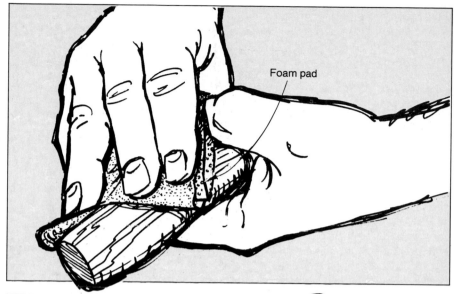

Foam pad

Finish-sanding pads

Are you having trouble finding just the right kind of sanding pad for effectively finish-sanding contoured shapes?

TIP: We found that foam paint and varnish brushes of various sizes make excellent backing pads for use with fine-grit sandpapers. Remove the handle and wrap the paper around the pad. The thin, flexible pads provide firm backing for uniform sanding, yet allow the paper to follow the contours of the piece you're working on.

—From the *WOOD* magazine shop

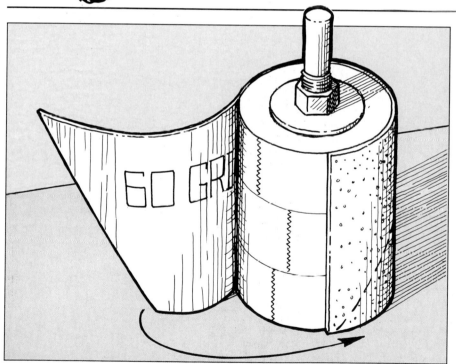

60 GRI

Slip-sliding away no more

Small workpieces can be hard to clamp or fasten to the work-bench for sanding or planing.

TIP: Use double-faced tape to secure strips of used sanding belts—the coarser, the better—to your workbench top. The sandpaper helps keep pieces of wood stationary while you safely sand or plane them. This trick works especially well if you need both hands to operate the tool.

—From the *WOOD* magazine shop

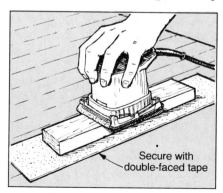

Secure with double-faced tape

One way to beat the (sanding) drum

Being in the middle of a project and finding out you don't have the right size or grit of sanding sleeves for a drum can be frustrating.

TIP: Cover the drum with double-faced carpet tape, leaving the protective film in place. Then, cut a strip of sandpaper of the correct width and taper one end at an angle. Fit in place, penciling a line where the ends meet. Cut so the sandpaper ends butt together. Remove the tape's protective strip and affix the sandpaper.

—Thomas P. Rockey, Northfield, Minn.

Sanding

Know when to stop sanding

It's all too easy to sand through the thin veneer of plywood and fibercore lumber when belt-sanding a finished frame edge, whether in a cabinet or a picture frame. Sanding frames that mount to the bottom of a few recent-model belt sanders help, but what if you don't own such an accessory?

TIP: Shade a wavy pencil line on the veneer edge that butts up against the frame. Stop sanding the joint just after the pencil line disappears. The same technique works well on banded tops and shelves.

—Terry Leach, Lovington, Ill.

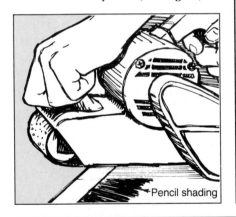
Pencil shading

Spotting sanding gouges

When smoothing a surface with a belt sander, it's difficult to tell if you've gouged the wood by tipping the sander or created cross-grain scratches by moving the machine sideways.

TIP: Clamp a small portable light to your work surface so that it illuminates the piece being sanded from a low angle. By sighting along the light, you'll be able to spot even the slightest dip (it will show up as a shadow among the highlights).

This technique also works for illuminating various depths of a relief carving.

—From the *WOOD* magazine shop

Special sanding blocks

Homemade sanding blocks tend to wear out quickly and may not do a clean job in corners. Holding the paper in place can cramp your fingers and a good deal of the sandpaper surface isn't used. There just has to be a better way.

TIP: Use the same sanding belts you use on your belt sander to do the job. Cut ¾" or 1" material equal to the width and one-half the total length of the belt. If necessary, insert a shim or wedge to tighten the belt. Use the same block to quickly change grits of sandpaper.

—Doug Lodin, Brooklyn Center, Minn.

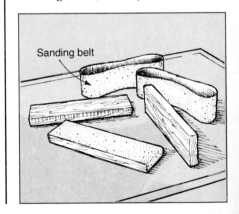
Sanding belt

Clamps help you sand edges

Hand-holding a belt sander to finish the edge of one or more pieces of stock can turn into a balancing act. Here's a dependable way to do it and make the boards an even width at the same time.

TIP: Hold the pieces together with handscrew clamps as shown at *right* and secure one end of the assembly to the benchtop with a third clamp. This arrangement gives you a wide, stable surface to sand, and ensures uniform sanding of the material. If you have only one board to sand, clamp auxiliary scrap boards of equal or longer size to its sides to support the sander.

—Charlotte Arthur, Colbert, Okla.

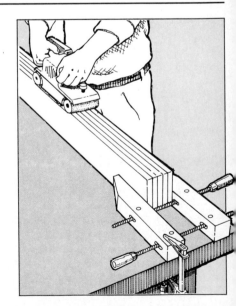

Sanding

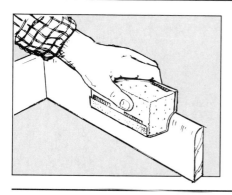

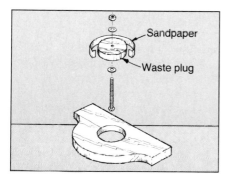

Sand the hole thing
Hole cutters are great for their intended use, but sanding the inside of the circle is a pain.

TIP: Use the waste plug from the hole to build a custom drum sander. Cut a $1/32$"-wide slot about $3/8$" deep into the side of the plug. Cut a piece of sandpaper the thickness of the plug by the circumference plus $3/4$". Slip a bolt through the plug's hole, and tighten a nut on the back side. Chuck this sander in your drill and sand as desired.
—**Rusty McKnight, Gadsden, Tenn.**

Sanding shortcut
Sanding those small, commercially available spindles can consume a lot of time and sandpaper.

TIP: Use a drill press to speed this process. Place one end of the spindle in the chuck (finger-tighten only). Then drive a No. 6 finishing nail through a piece of scrap and place the scrap (nailhead side down) on the drill-press table. Secure with a C-clamp. Each end of the spindle should have a small hole where attached to the lathe. Lower the spindle hole over the nail, turn on the drill press, and sand.
—**Richard J. Wessels, St. Louis Park, Minn.**

Pliable sanding blocks
It's darn-near impossible to evenly sand the surface of millwork, such as quarter-round or cove molding, with conventional flat-faced sanding blocks. Sponge-backed abrasives help, but may not sand evenly.

TIP: Custom-make sanding blocks for specific jobs, using scraps of polystyrene foam (used for packing material or insulation). Carve or press the foam to the desired shape and fasten sandpaper with double-sided carpet tape. The blocks then fit anything you wish to sand and they're easy to make as you go along.
—**Norm Pedersen, Salt Lake City**

Narrow sanding belt reaches tight spots
One-inch-wide sanding belts do an excellent job of smoothing a variety of wood surfaces, including gentle curves. But when it comes to constricted openings and some small workpieces, an inch-wide belt may be too wide.

TIP: Slit the belt in half lengthwise to create a ½"-wide sanding belt. Start by piercing the center back side of the belt with a sharp knife. Then grab the sanding belt on both sides and tear down the center as shown at *right*.
—**Terry Fenimore, Waukee, Iowa**

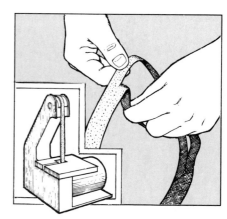

Sanding

Customized drum sanders at a fraction of the cost

Drum sanders are super for smoothing concave curves, but sometimes the drums and sleeves you have just don't match the job. Have you ever considered making your own?

TIP: Making your own drums can save you a trip to the hardware store and a fistful of change while suiting the job to a tee. Here's what you need: A replacement core, such as a length of mailing tube or the center from a roll of paper toweling, two circular pieces of wood with a slight taper, a threaded rod, nuts, washers, and sawdust. Assemble as shown in the drawing, packing the tube with sawdust. Tightening the ends compresses the sawdust, adding firmness to the spindle. Finally, cover the drum with sandpaper, securing it with glue or double-faced tape.

—Gregg Lehman, Rochester, N.Y.

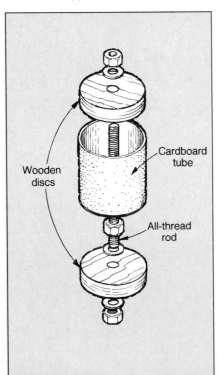

Wooden discs

Cardboard tube

All-thread rod

Avoid sanding gouges

Catching the power cord of a belt sander on the edge of a workpiece while you're sanding almost guarantees an ugly gouge (and a worn cord).

TIP: Drape the cord over your shoulder to keep it up and out of the way and to prevent sudden halts.

—From the *WOOD* magazine shop

In-the-groove sanding keeps you looking sharp

Sanding often wears away fine grooves and sharp edges in wood instead of making them look more attractive.

TIP: When you want to retain or define a sharp line or edge while sanding V-grooves in a project, wrap your sandpaper over the edge of a cabinet scraper. Sand one side first, as shown, and then the opposite side.

—From the *WOOD* magazine shop

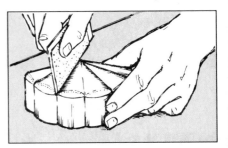

Help for sanding midget parts

Attempting to use a vertical belt sander on miniature parts is difficult—and even dangerous—because of the comparatively wide gap between the edge of the sander's table and the belt.

TIP: Clamp an auxiliary top of 1″ wood stock or plywood onto the existing table, leaving zero clearance between the sanding belt and the new working surface. This will fully support the workpieces.

—From the *WOOD* magazine shop

Scrollsaw aids

A sandwich for cutting thin metal and veneer

It's difficult to make good, clean cuts in thin metal, plastic, or veneer with a scrollsaw or bandsaw because the flimsy material may bend or even get caught in the saw blade. And, your fingers can easily slip on the thin stock as you maneuver it. As a consequence you might ruin the stock or possibly injure yourself.

TIP: Place the thin material between two pieces of plywood or similar thin stock, held together with dabs of five-minute epoxy or hotmelt adhesive as shown at *right, above.* Before assembling the sandwich, drill $1/16$" holes at the corners of the thin material so you'll know its position inside the plywood pieces. Tape or glue the cutting pattern to the bottom side of the assembly as shown at *right,* and then flip the piece over before you start cutting. If you've made vertical cuts, the pattern portion should drop out cleanly.

—From the *WOOD* magazine shop

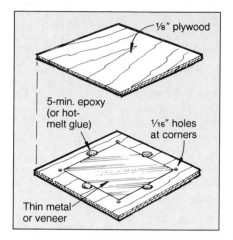

1/8" plywood

5-min. epoxy (or hot-melt glue)

1/16" holes at corners

Thin metal or veneer

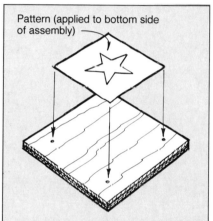

Pattern (applied to bottom side of assembly)

Extra life for blades

Normally, only about one-third of the length of a scrollsaw blade is used. When that section becomes dull, nearly two-thirds of the blade remains sharp.

TIP: Make use of the other two-thirds of the blade with an auxiliary table of a thickness of your choosing. For instance, make the auxiliary table $3/4$" thick if you cut a lot of $3/4$" stock. Clamp this spacer to the table of your scrollsaw, or attach it with double-faced tape. This attachment limits the thickness of the material you can cut, but in most cases, the stock will be thin.

—Elvin Perry, Manteca, Calif.

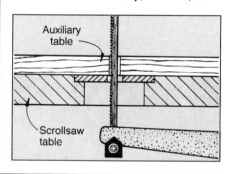

Auxiliary table

Scrollsaw table

Smoother scrolling

If you've ever used a scrollsaw to cut intricate pieces from stock $1/8$" or thinner, you've probably noticed that it's hard to negotiate sharp curves and still stay on the line. It's also tough to get a clean cut.

TIP: We've found it's much easier to make tight cuts in stock at least $1/2$" thick because the blade cuts less aggressively, giving you better control. Also, it's easier to hold and control the stock with your fingers. So, when working with thin material, tape several pieces together and stack-cut them. Need only one? Tape the thin stock to a scrap of $1/2$" knot-free softwood.

—From the *WOOD* magazine shop

Small-Stock Handling

Clever ways to surface thin strips

Surfacing the faces of thin or narrow lengths of exotic woods is simple enough if you have the luxury of owning a thickness planer. But what if you have only a 6" jointer?

TIP: With hotmelt adhesive, spot-weld the strip to be surfaced to the square edge of a board that's approximately as wide as the workpiece. Now, feed the material safely through the jointer until you reach the desired thickness. (It helps to take thin cuts.) You can separate the pieces with a wooden wedge, provided you apply the hotmelt adhesive sparingly in small spots, not long beads.

—John A. Byer, Vancouver, British Columbia

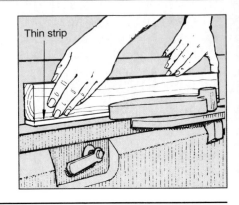

Clothespins become mighty micro-clamps

Putting together tiny projects, such as dollhouse furniture, wooden models, or jewelry, can get awfully frustrating, especially when you're gluing fragile, intricate parts.

TIP: Reshape spring-activated wooden clothespins into miniature clamps as shown *above*. You can tailor their tips to fit different situations. The softwood pins won't damage delicate surfaces.

—John Monaghan, Goleta, Calif.

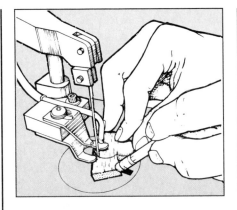

Control small pieces with a pencil

Scrollsawing parts from small pieces of stock can be tricky business because the blade action tends to lift the workpiece off the cutting table.

TIP: Press the workpiece against the saw's table with the eraser end of a pencil as shown *above* to guide the workpiece. The rubber tip grips the part to help you control it and follow the cutting line.

—Louis Mouis, Aurora, Ill.

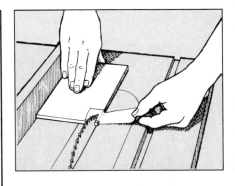

Rip narrow strips safely

Ripping short, narrow strips of wood on a tablesaw can be dangerous. Once you complete the cut, the loose strip could bind between the blade and rip fence, creating a kickback hazard.

TIP: Set up your saw so you can cut the strip on the outside of the blade rather than between the blade and the rip fence. Stabilize the strip by adding a 6–8"-long piece of at least ¾"-wide masking tape or' duct tape so you can snatch the piece away from the blade when you finish the cut. *Caution: Be sure the blade guard is in place when making this kind of cut; we omitted it from the drawing only for the sake of clarity.*

If you need several strips the same size, make a pencil mark on the table. Then, align the outside edge of the piece being cut and move the fence for each successive cut.

—From the *WOOD* magazine shop

Follow some basic lines on your saw table

Aligning the miter-gauge fence truly perpendicular to the blade of your tablesaw can be pretty iffy, especially if you're in a hurry. Similarly, accurately setting a 45° angle on a miter gauge can be a time-consuming task.

TIP: Clamp a carpenter's square at a right angle to the miter-gauge groove, *top drawing, at right,* and score a fine line in the surface of the table with a steel scriber. Next, clamp the square in place so the legs of the square are equally long, *middle drawing,* and scribe another line that intersects the first one at 45°. Finally, flip over the square, clamp it in place at the correct diagonal, and scribe a third time. This provides you with accurate reference lines for quickly setting your miter gauge at the three most common angles.

—From the *WOOD* magazine shop

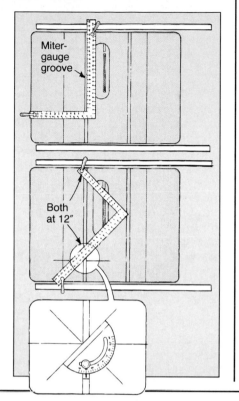

Improved miter stop

Sawdust buildup at a tablesaw miter stop can produce uneven lengths of pieces.

TIP: Cut a ⅛ × ⅛" notch in the block of wood used for a miter stop. In addition to solving the inevitable problem of sawdust buildup, the notch allows more freedom for the point of the mitered piece to fit snugly against the stop.

—From the *WOOD* magazine shop

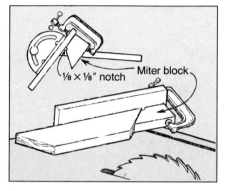

Precise miter cuts every time

Accurately setting the miter gauge on a tablesaw for an odd-degree cut, such as 22½° from center, is nearly impossible without the help of a measuring tool such as an adjustable triangle. You can buy such an instrument for about $10, or you can be just as accurate with much more common materials.

TIP: You'll need a protractor, scissors, pencil, straightedge, and sheet of heavy paper or thin poster board. First, mark a point about halfway across the bottom edge of the piece of paper. Then, lay the protractor along that edge, with its center over the marked point you just made. Now, mark a second point at the outside of the protractor at the desired number of degrees from the 90° mark as shown in Step 1 *above.* For this example, since

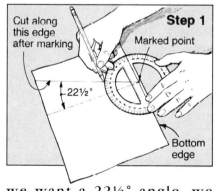

we want a 22½° angle, we marked the second point at 67½° (90° minus 22½°). Connect the two points with a straight line that goes across the page, and use scissors to cut along the line, following it closely for maximum accuracy.

Moving to your tablesaw, keep the same face of the paper up and place its bottom edge away from the blade, with the just-cut edge facing the miter gauge. Move the edge nearest

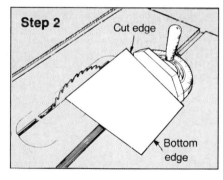

the blade flush against it and align the fence of the miter gauge with the cut edge as shown in Step 2 *above.* You can set the miter gauge for the same number of degrees from the other side of center by simply flipping the sheet over and placing the base edge along the blade. You may want to apply the piece of paper to a sheet of hardboard and cut it to shape for future use as a template.

—Ray Russell, Des Moines

Tablesaw Tactics

An accurate bevel that's on the level

The trick to cutting an accurate bevel on a long piece of stock is to keep the board flat against the surface of the tablesaw. If either end of the board raises off the table even slightly, the bevel will be uneven.

TIP: Attach a long, straight board to your fence. (Many fences have predrilled holes for this purpose.) Before gluing a piece of wood to the underside of the leading edge, be sure you can still use the fence-tightening knobs. This jig will help keep the stock aligned as the material feeds into the saw. Use a roller support on the outfeed.

—**Tom Peters, Midland, Mich.**

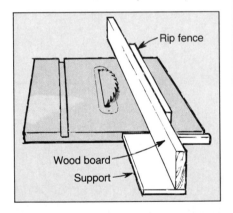

Rip fence

Wood board

Support

Splinter-free dadoing on the tablesaw

It's all too easy to chip the thin veneers covering plywoods when you use dado blades and a dado-blade insert on your tablesaw.

TIP: Make your own insert that will undergird the plywood (or any other workpiece) with support and reduce chipping. With a scrollsaw, bandsaw, or jigsaw, cut out an insert blank from the correct thickness of plywood or solid stock (use the original insert for a pattern). After you've mounted the blade, install and secure the blank. Then raise the blade to the proper cutting height. Now you will be cutting with maximum support.

—**Arnold J. Schafer, Yakima, Wash.**

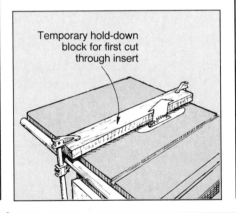

Temporary hold-down block for first cut through insert

Oh nuts★!★!★ There it goes again

Once again you're digging through mounds of sawdust to find the arbor nut you dropped while changing blades on your tablesaw. Help!

TIP: Slip the nut onto your index finger. Then, while controlling the nut with your thumb and middle finger, place the tip of your index finger on the arbor shaft. Keep your index finger in contact with the arbor and spin the nut with your middle finger and thumb.

—**From the *WOOD* magazine shop**

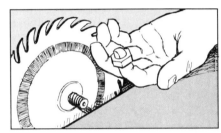

A safe strategy for cutting small pieces

Cutting small pieces of stock on a tablesaw or router always is a challenge. Safely cutting the ends of pieces can leave you a bundle of nerves.

TIP: Make a right-angle jig block like the one shown from plywood and clamp the small piece to the jig. The jig also serves as a chip breaker—an advantage over a tenoning jig, which doesn't follow behind the workpiece as this jig does.

—**From the *WOOD* magazine shop**

Parallel check for rip fence

Even with normal, careful use, tablesaw ripping guides, meant to be parallel with the saw blade, become misaligned. As a result, sawn pieces don't fit perfectly because they contain practically undetectable tapers.

TIP: Routinely check alignment by setting the guide a few inches from the saw blade and tightening or locking it in place. Measure the distances between the nearest miter-gauge slot, both at the front and back of the table. If the fence is out of adjustment, reset until distances are equal, front and back.

Zero-clearance blade slot

Narrow stock is pulled into your tablesaw's insert during ripping, and extra-thin pieces kickback.

TIP: With the tablesaw blade in the fully lowered position, clamp a hardboard piece firmly to the saw top. Turn the saw on and very slowly raise the blade to working height. After it has cut its way through the hardboard, the saw blade will have zero clearance. The hardboard also serves to support thin stock.

—From the *WOOD* magazine shop

Large trim guide

Few of us own tablesaws capable of safely and accurately crosscutting large workpieces. Or do we?

TIP: Use the saw-table edge as a guide. Clamp a 1×6 to the underside of the material the appropriate distance away from, and parallel to, the intended cut-off line. Then, run it through the saw, using the 1×6 as your fence. Use this technique to straighten an uneven edge, too.

—From the *WOOD* magazine shop

Be sure to do the following maintenance chore periodically too: Loosen the screws that connect the beam of the ripping guide to its front end. Lay the beam so one edge lies exactly along one side of a miter gauge slot and snug the guide in place. Now tighten the screws.

—From the *WOOD* magazine shop

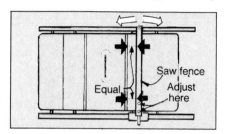

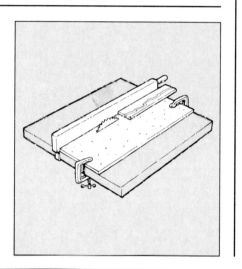

All doweled up and no way to cut it

A dowel's cylindrical shape is both a blessing and a curse. It makes the material a remarkably versatile woodworking resource for countless jobs around the shop. But, working a cylindrical object can be frustrating because it just won't stay put.

TIP: This handy jig, a scrap 2×4 with a hole the diameter of the dowel bored through it, makes dadoing, trimming to length, or decreasing the diameter of a dowel a safe and simple procedure on your radial-arm or tablesaw. Drive a finish nail through the 2×4 and just far enough into the dowel to prevent it from turning.

—From the *WOOD* magazine shop

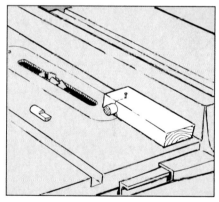

Tablesaw Tactics

Handy blade-height gauges

Measuring the depth of cut for various wood thicknesses on a tablesaw involves a lot of adjusting and readjusting.

TIP: Gather scraps of plywood or other stock in common thicknesses you normally use, then cut them into uniform squares. Label each for permanent reference. Keep them handy by drilling a hole in each and hanging on a peg, or string them up necklace-style. They're a real time-saver in any shop.

—From the *WOOD* magazine shop

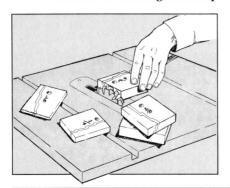

Miter nice

The slick metal surface of a miter gauge often is the cuplrit when wood slides into the tablesaw blade.

TIP: To prevent wood from sliding, use double-faced tape to affix medium- or fine-grit sandpaper to the face of the miter gauge of any power tool. You can easily replace the tape and sandpaper when necessary.

—Bill Roberts, Angola, Ind.

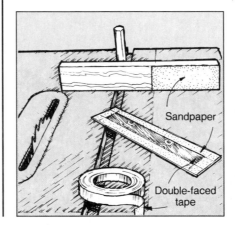

Sandpaper

Double-faced tape

Tablesaw sanding disc

A good stationary disc sander can turn the drudgery of sanding into an easy job. But, if you can't afford one, get ready for tedious hours of sanding.

TIP: Cut an 8″ circle out of ¼″ tempered hardboard and bore a hole the size of your tablesaw's arbor in the exact center (usually ⅝″). Use spray adhesive to attach 80-grit sandpaper to one side and 100-grit to the other. Mount the disc in place of the tablesaw blade.

—From the *WOOD* magazine shop

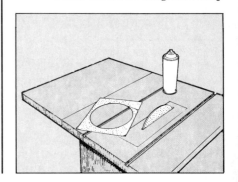

Paraffin helps your rip fence glide smoothly

The metal parts of a ripping fence and the rail on which it rides can stick, making it difficult to position the fence exactly as you want.

TIP: Rub a paraffin bar along the rail as shown at *right* to apply a thin coat of wax, which allows the fence to glide smoothly along the rail. You can purchase paraffin at most grocery stores.

—From the *WOOD* magazine shop

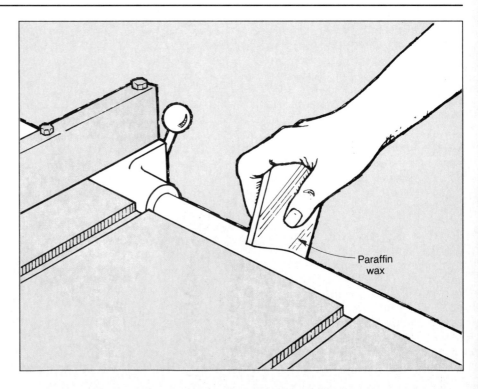

Paraffin wax

Tablesaw Tactics

Check your miter-gauge pointer for accuracy

Most tablesaw miter gauges have an adjustable pointer for setting the gauge. Accidentally dropping the miter gauge may knock the pointer out of alignment, or vibration can loosen the setscrew so the pointer no longer gives you a correct reading. In any event, your pointer should be checked for accuracy.

TIP: To check the trueness of your miter gauge, set it for a square cut and crosscut a short length of 6″-wide board, holding it snugly against the miter gauge as shown in drawing 1 at *right*. We exaggerated an out-of-square cut for clarity.

Now, flip the board end for end and make a similar cut. If the gauge is set correctly, both edges of the board will be the same length ("A" and "B" shown in drawing 2 at *right* would be equal). A difference of ⅟₁₆″ between "A" and "B" on a 6″-wide board indicates the angle is 0.3° out of square. The wider the board you use, the more accurate the measurement becomes. Correct misalignment by resetting the gauge, adjusting the pointer, and repeating this procedure to check accuracy of your readjustment.

—F.V. Chmielowiec, Boulder, Colo.

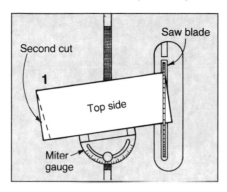

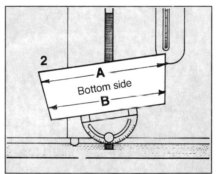

Hang your gear here

Finding a place to lay your tablesaw wrench and miter gauge presents a challenge in everyone's shop. Too often they fall or get pushed to the floor and need to be recalibrated, too.

TIP: Use hooks designed for perforated hardboard to keep tablesaw accessories right at your fingertips. Drill two ³⁄₁₆″ holes about 1″ apart on the side of the saw. Because of the flat surface, straight hooks are best for the miter gauge; curved hooks are suitable for securing the wrench.

—Richard J. Wessels, St. Louis Park, Minn.

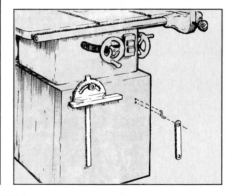

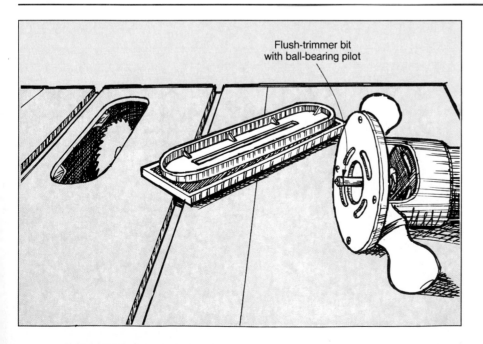

Flush-trimmer bit with ball-bearing pilot

Table inserts a snap to make with help of a trimming bit

Despite the accuracy of dado and molding blades, distorted cuts can occur when the workpiece is not completely supported by the table insert.

TIP: You can make several table inserts with a router and thin plywood scraps. With double-faced tape, join the metal dado insert with a rough-sawn plywood blank. Cut the plywood to the exact size with a laminate flush trimmer in your router. Keep several blanks on hand for a variety of tasks. The zero-clearance cutting increases operator safety, too.

—Michael Cosgrove, Goose Creek, S.C.

Tool Maintenance

Sharpening with a drill press

Putting the proper bevel on chisels and plane blades isn't an easy freehand skill.

TIP: Use a drill press and drum-sander attachment with appropriate grit sleeves to grind blades. Clamp the blade or chisel in a drill-press vise with the blade perpendicular to the table and parallel to the quill. Position and secure the vise to the table with a C-clamp. With the sander turning slowly, raise and lower the quill to sharpen the blade. To move the blade closer to the drum, tap the vise with a mallet. Work slowly to prevent excessive heat buildup.

—J.J. Sawyer, Pensacola, Fla.

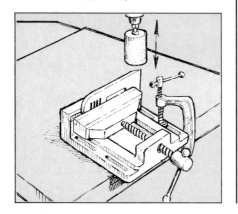

Drill-bit maintenance

After several uses, large-diameter bits often slip around in the drill chuck and create burrs on the bit shaft. Large burrs may prevent the bit from fitting squarely in the chuck.

TIP: A mill-bastard file quickly removes the burrs. Support the bit on a flat surface with part of the shaft overhanging the edge, as shown *below*. Slowly rotate the bit as you file. The same technique also restores damaged router bits.

—From the *WOOD* magazine shop

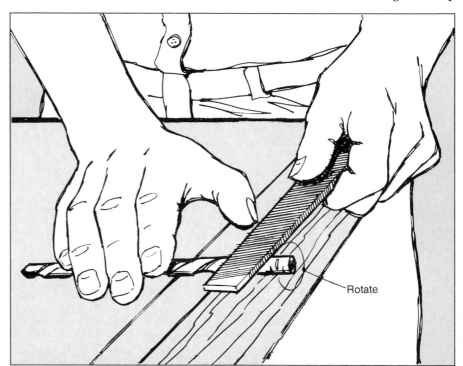

Rotate

Stay charged up

The cordless drill is a super convenience—unless you regularly use one all day long. Prolonged operation runs down the battery, meaning you have to stop drilling while it recharges.

TIP: When you buy a cordless drill, invest a few more dollars in an extra battery pack. This allows you to continue drilling while the other battery pack recharges. Now you can drill for hours on end and never have to stop in the middle of a job for lack of a charge.

—Dan Miller, Elgin, Ill.

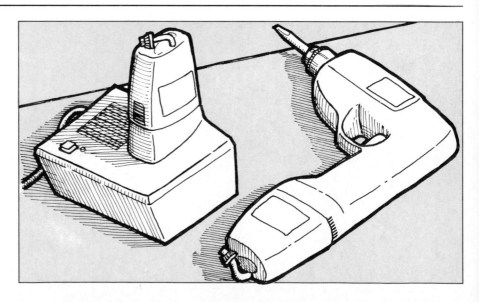

Tool Maintenance

Felt bad about marring
Oops! You've just pulled another nail from a piece of wood and remembered, too late, how easily a hammerhead dents the wood surface.

TIP: Glue a piece of felt or apply adhesive-backed felt to the top of the hammer. It's dependable and much easier than searching for a scrap of wood when removing nails.

—Al Bruder, Chicago

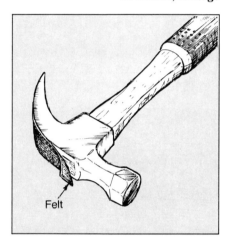

Felt

How to lick gooey stickers
Who likes to pick away at a hard-to-remove gummed label on a new tool handle or other item, then tediously clean off the gummy residue?

TIP: Before peeling, hit the label with a few squirts of WD-40 lubricant. It quickly dissolves the gum adhesive, so you can easily peel off the label. A quick wipe with a rag will remove any remaining goo. *Caution: Don't try this on unfinished wood. It may leave a residue.*

—Joseph White, Altus, Okla.

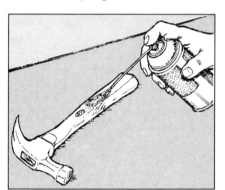

"Tackful" way to clean face shields
Irritating fine sawdust accumulates on face shields and goggles and reduces visibility.

TIP: Inexpensive tack cloths wipe a shield clean in a hurry. Tack cloths will not create static and attract more dust—a frequent complaint about some wiping cloths. Keep a tack cloth handy just for this task.

—Donald Christianson, Green Bay, Wis.

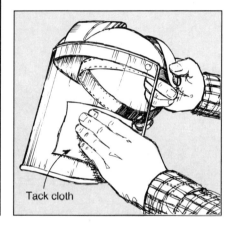

Tack cloth

Surform sharpening
The Stanley Surform and similar forming tools work great, but the blades eventually dull.

TIP: Sharpen these blades with the small stones used for pocket knives. Rows of teeth run diagonally across the length of the blade, and each row has a "lead side" with cutting edges near the top. Hold the stone firmly against the inside face of the lead side and run the stone back and forth through each groove. Between sharpenings, the blade can be renewed by running a stone along the length of the blade in the direction the cutting faces are pointing.

—Mary Butcher, Hacienda Heights, Calif.

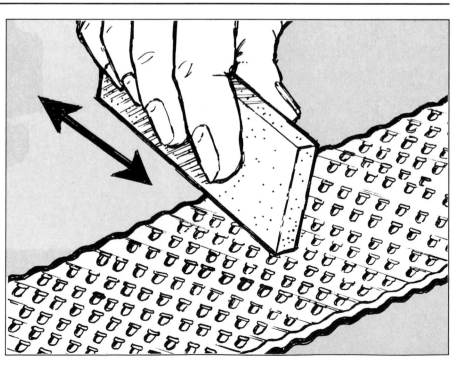

Tool Maintenance

An idea fresh from the oven

Accumulated pitch and gum on saw blades and router bits speeds the dulling process.

TIP: Oven cleaner is an effective, safe, and inexpensive pitch and tar remover. In addition, oven cleaner is less volatile than lighter fluids used for the same purpose by some woodworkers.

—Mike Innis, Atlanta

Clamp care tip

Glue squeeze-out sometimes dries and adheres to the face of handscrew clamps. Later, projects that have been clamped turn out with marred surfaces because of dried-on glue globs.

TIP: Apply a coat of paste wax to the face of each jaw of your clamps to prevent glue buildup. It's also a good idea to maintain a light coat of wax on metal clamps—this will help you prevent rust from forming and discoloring project surfaces.

—Carl Scholl, Mancelona, Mich.

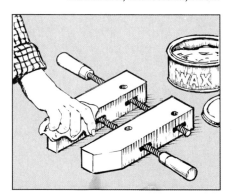

Sprucing up metal tops

The top of your tablesaw looks forlorn—blemished by minor stains or corrosion. And, your jointer beds are coated with crud accumulated from jointing hundreds of boards.

TIP: Brighten their appearance by spraying with rust remover or WD-40, then scouring with No. 3 steel wool pads on a pad sander (orbital action works best). Surfaces will shine like new after a few minutes' work. But don't saturate the sanders' felt pad.

—From the *WOOD* magazine shop

Leveling with a wire

Squaring up a tilting table on a drill press so it's perpendicular to a drill bit can prove tedious.

TIP: Instead of using a square, a small length of coat hanger will do the job quickly and accurately. Cut a length of wire approximately 6″ long, and bend right angles in it as shown. Don't worry if the angles aren't exactly 90°. Chuck one end into the drill and tighten. Raise the table so it touches the wire. Slowly rotate the drill chuck 180° by hand so you can detect any high or low spots in the table.

—John Clark, Cuddebackville, N.Y.

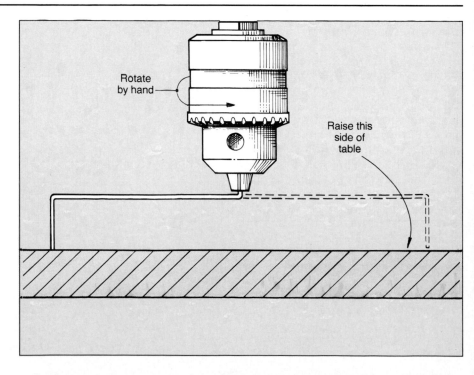

Rotate by hand

Raise this side of table

Just the solution to workshop noise pollution

Vibrating metal power-tool bases, stands, and cabinets create a lot of noise and can really frazzle your nerves after a while. Does this mean you have to build better stands? Hardly.

TIP: Here's how you can cut out a lot of that noise permanently in short order. Disassemble the stand or base and apply a bead of good, low-shrinkage construction adhesive—Franklin's Premium 5661 is one brand—anywhere metal parts touch. When it's reassembled, you should notice quite a substantial reduction in noise when the machine runs.

—Robert M. Vaughan, Roanoke, Va.

Construction adhesive

Slick care for clamps

Even tidy woodworkers get dried-on globs of glue on their pipe and bar clamps from squeeze-out and smearing.

TIP: Clean up your clamps and rub a thick layer of paraffin or paste wax over all parts. After that, the dried glue deposits will peel or chip off easily. Reapply the lubricant occasionally.

—Glen Miller, Morristown, Minn.

PASTE WAX

Static-cling cure helps you win the war on dust

Powder-fine sawdust that accumulates and sticks to face shields, goggles, and glasses can interfere with a safe, clear view of your work when using power tools. The culprit: static electricity that builds up on everything in a workshop with dry air.

TIP: Put the kibosh on static electricity by cleaning your safety eyewear with a used sheet of fabric softener. Fresh pieces contain a heavier chemical and are not as soft as those that have been through the clothes dryer at least once. The soft sheet will remove both dust and static without scratching the lenses. If you don't have any fabric softener sheets, a thin film of Armor All brand automotive vinyl protectant rubbed in with a soft cloth also works well.

You can also use this trick to clean and treat clear plastic shields on power tools. Repeat the treatment as necessary.

—Anita K. Booth, Lakewood, Calif.

Tool Maintenance

Here's an idea that's easy to warm up to

Removing old sandpaper attached to disc sanders with pressure-sensitive glue can become a headache, especially when the adhesive won't release. Eventually, the paper tears and pulls apart and leaves a mess on the metal mounting plate. There has to be an easier way!

TIP: Use heat to soften the adhesive. The source can be a handheld hair dryer as shown *below,* a heat gun, or even a heat lamp. Apply heat directly to the sanding disc in a waving motion that covers the entire disc. Test by lifting the disc, and use more heat if necessary.

—**Steve E. Miller, Dallas, Ore.**

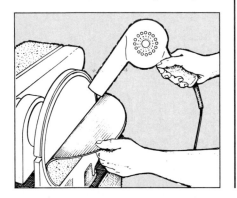

Radial-arm sharpening jig

Chisel and plane blades are tough to hone because they require a hollow or concave bevel that keeps edges sharp. Even if you use a grinder it's hard to be consistently true.

TIP: Build a jig as shown, from plywood or other scrap and two bolts fitted with wing nuts. Fasten a grinding wheel to your radial-arm saw, then adjust the position of the jig and the grinding wheel height to achieve the proper angle. Controlled passing of the radial arm does the rest.

—**From the *WOOD* magazine shop**

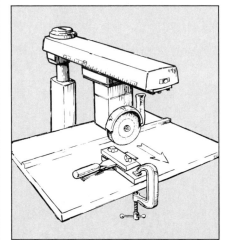

A safe way to sharpen a scraper

Skinned knuckles and sharp hand scrapers go together when you use a vise to hold the scraper for filing. One slip is all it takes. That smarts!

TIP: Clamp a fine single-cut bastard file horizontally in the vise as shown *below.* While holding the scraper perpendicular to the file, draw it back with firm, even pressure. It only takes two or three strokes. Now you're ready to scrape away.

—**Edwin C. Trefz, Norwood, Pa.**

(You can also turn over the edges of a newly sharpened scraper by securing a burnisher in the vise.)

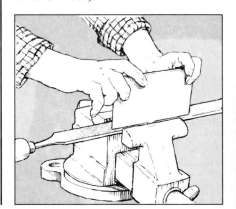

Rx for balky tape measures

With extended use, metal tape measures get gummed up and no longer retract smoothly. Moreover, the painted markings wear thin.

TIP: Pull the tape all the way out and apply a thin coat of auto body wax to both sides. When you roll up the tape, the wax will protect the markings on the face of the tape while lubricating the inner mechanism so it works smoothly. Reapply the wax from time to time.

—**D. Roboway, Winnipeg, Manitoba**

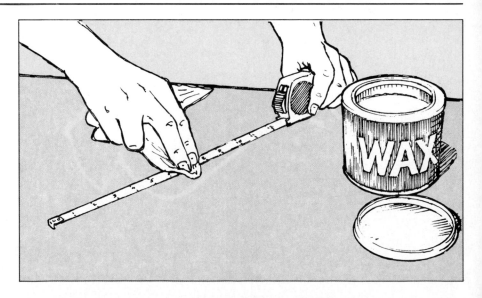

Tool Maintenance

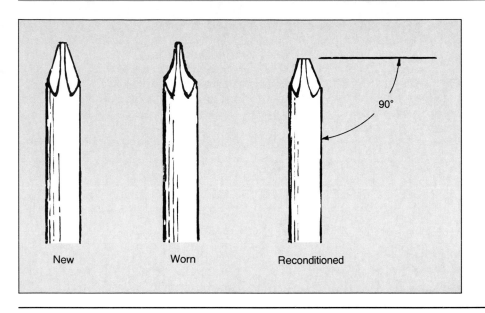

New

Worn

Reconditioned

90°

Tune up your Phillips

With use, the tips of Phillips screwdrivers wear down so the fin-like blades become ragged and hard to keep seated. One of these tools in disrepair may pop out of the slots and disfigure the screwhead or the surrounding wood surface.

TIP: Recondition the screwdriver by carefully filing or grinding off the tip with a flat file and touching up the blades with a three-corner file so the whole tip seats snugly into screwheads. As you work, check the fit with a Phillips screw.

—From the *WOOD* magazine shop

First aid for your dull jigsaw blades

Halfway through a "must-do" project, you discover that the blade on your jigsaw is dull, and you don't have a spare.

TIP: Touch up the blade with a triangular file. Place the blade in a vise with teeth pointing up (don't pinch them). File away from you, giving each tooth two or three quick strokes. Rotate the blade 180°, and file the other side in a similar fashion.

—From the *WOOD* magazine shop

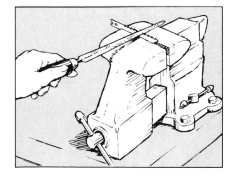

Sander belt revitalizer

Sander belts clog up quickly and need replacing.

TIP: An old, hard, crepe-soled shoe heel does a great job of removing resin and sawdust buildup. Hold it against the moving belt and watch the belt come clean.

—From the *WOOD* magazine shop

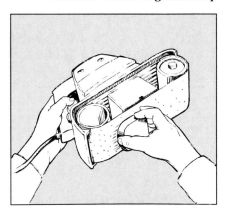

Brush away buildup

Resin and contact adhesive build up on router bits, reducing cutting efficiency.

TIP: To clean yours, apply lighter fluid, or gum and pitch remover, and scrub them with a toothbrush. Apply periodically to keep your bits sparkling.

—From the *WOOD* magazine shop

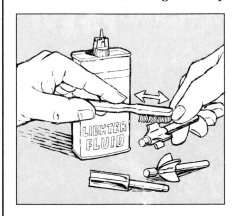

Turning

Screw center to the rescue

You want to cut wood, not metal, but it's sometimes difficult to avoid dinging your lathe tools against the faceplate while turning the entire profile of a piece. You also encounter this frustration when you turn small pieces such as knobs.

TIP: Make a wooden screw center or first screw your workpiece to a wooden disc, then attach either to the faceplate. Now you have a wooden buffer plate between the workpiece and the metal faceplate to eliminate those dings. If your faceplate isn't drilled for a center screw, mount the plywood washer to the center of the project with a wood screw; attach the disc to the faceplate as usual. If your faceplate is drilled for a center screw, fasten directly through the faceplate and disc and into your project.

—Sean O'Daniel, Lebanon, Ky.

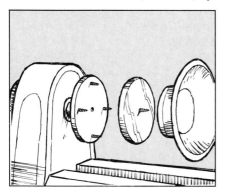

Tape gives stiff upper lip to turned bowls

It's a challenge to turn a wooden bowl with thin walls and remove interior stock without cracking or breaking the bowl's outside edge.

TIP: After turning the lip of the bowl, reinforce the lip with a strip of masking tape before turning the rest of the interior. Make sure the tape doesn't unravel by wrapping it in the direction opposite of the rotation of your lathe.

—David Arnall, Berkeley Vale, New South Wales, Australia

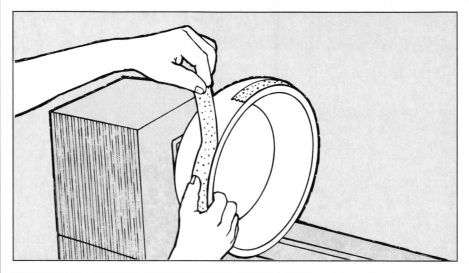

Spin balance in the shop

No matter how meticulous you are, the four wooden wheels you make in your shop each have their own characteristics and never perform as a set. How can you make them uniform?

TIP: Here's a solution that solves this problem and also saves time: First, use a hole saw to cut the wheels from your favorite stock. Slip a ¼″ bolt through the center of the wheels and tighten with nuts at each end of the stack. Then, sand all the wheels at once.

—Stephen R. Garavatti, Salt Lake City

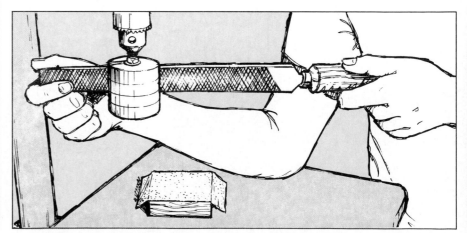

Slick solution

Thread-on faceplates sometimes tend to lock to the live spindle of a lathe and this makes them difficult to remove.

TIP: Before you screw on the faceplate, slip on a single layer of waxed paper and tighten the faceplate to the live spindle as usual. The waxed paper "washer" will make it easier to loosen the faceplate.

—**From the *WOOD* magazine shop**

A dust blaster to use on your lathe

Many power tools, including the lathe, produce mountains of irritating, fine wood dust. A dust-collection system often provides the ideal solution, but an expensive and noisy one.

TIP: To keep dust out of your eyes and nose while turning wood, build this slingshot-style fan that you can install in the outboard tool rest of your lathe. Cut the ¾"-thick yoke to fit a 4–5" axial fan typically used for cooling a computer or audio equipment. You can purchase the fans from electronic-supply stores for about $15. Screw together the yoke and a notched dowel of the appropriate size to fit the tool rest. Wire the fan with standard 14-gauge power cord, including a switch near the fan.

—**Rus Hurt, Port Wing, Wis.**

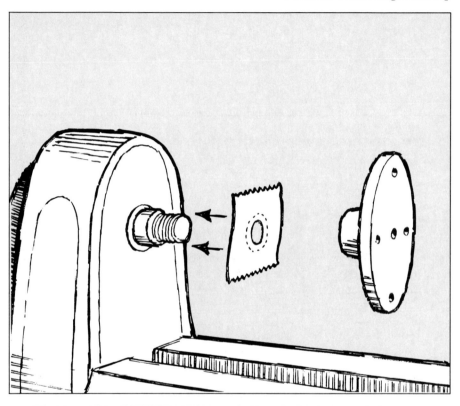

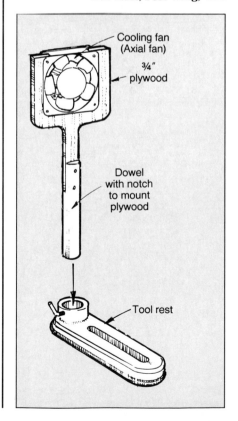

Cooling fan
(Axial fan)

¾"
plywood

Dowel
with notch
to mount
plywood

Tool rest

Catch that storm of lathe chips in its tracks

Turning wood on a lathe often generates a cloud of dust and fine chips that can nearly overcome you after a few minutes.

TIP: In a suitable length of 1 × 4" stock, cut a hole just large enough to receive the nozzle of your dust collector or shop vacuum. Place it underneath the piece being turned. If the size of your workpiece allows, make a box with the hose fitted near the bottom of the enclosure as shown in the bottom drawing.

—**Mark T. Jones, Durham, N.C.**

Turning

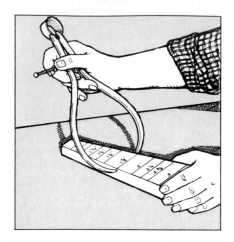

Set calipers quickly with this gauge
Constantly resetting calipers can prove to be a monotonous chore that requires a lot of time and poses the possibility of making incorrect settings.

TIP: Cut a piece of stock that tapers from ½″ to 3½″ wide for a gauge to set your calipers. Draw lines at widths you commonly use and label them as shown at *left*. This provides a quick gauge for flawlessly setting calipers.

—David L. Wiseley, Waters, Mich.

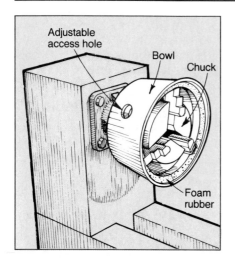

Adjustable access hole
Bowl
Chuck
Foam rubber

Muzzling a three-jawed chuck before it can bite
The jaw heels of some popular three-jawed chucks protrude enough to pose a real hazard to the operator whose knuckles or tools venture too close to the whirling edges.

TIP: Protect yourself with plastic tubs like the kind that hold margarine. Cut the bottom out of the tub and line the inside with foam-rubber weather stripping for a friction fit. With this installed, the shield will prevent you from getting whacked by the jaw heels, even if your knuckles get close enough for contact.

—David M. Lipscomb, Knoxville, Tenn.

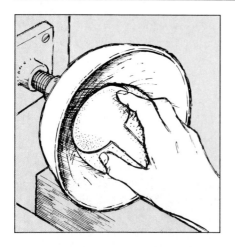

"On-the ball" sanding
Smoothly sanding the inside of bowls being turned on a lathe can be terribly frustrating as well as hard on the fingers.

TIP: Wrap sandpaper, emery cloth, or screen-type abrasives around a sponge rubber ball before you start. The ball fits the inside curvature, enabling you to do a more uniform job of sanding than you can do with hand-held sandpaper.

—Arthur Henrickson, Grand Rapids, Mich.

Workbench Improvements

A doggone good idea

Have you ever wished for a fancy cabinetmaker's bench, complete with steel bench dogs, but somehow couldn't justify the cost? Sure, you can fit steel dogs to your bench. But it's a hassle to cut the square mortises in the benchtop to accommodate them.

TIP: If your bench has a vise with pop-up stop, try this: Fit it with plastic dogs made for the Black & Decker Workmate. They cost less than steel dogs (about $1.25 each from Black & Decker dealers), and have *round* shanks. Drill a series of ¾" holes spaced a bit closer than the vise's widest opening in line with the center of your vise.

—Alan Shearer, Great Falls, Va.

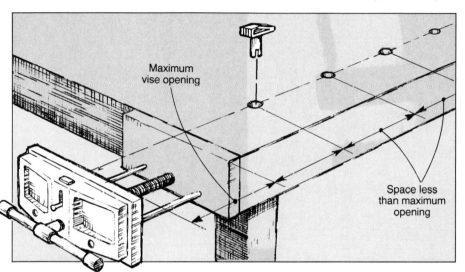

Maximum vise opening

Space less than maximum opening

Substitute bench dog

Bench dogs can be a woodworker's best friend, but not all workshop tables were created equal. How can you make your own substitute dogs?

TIP: There's an inexpensive way to build effective hold-down clamps for practically any workbench. Parallel rows of threaded inserts (try ⁵/₁₆" No. 18) placed across your table form this arrangement. As shown in the foreground of the drawing at *right*, two strips of wood, two

wedges, and four threaded rods and wing nuts complete the clamp. In the background, note how to clamp odd-shaped pieces using a block of wood under secured wood strips.

—John Wolf, St. Joseph, Mich.

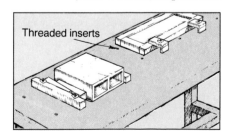

Threaded inserts

Bracket supports long stock at workbench

Many workbenches—homemade and commercial models alike—don't incorporate features to support long pieces protruding from the vise. As a result, it's necessary to scrounge around for an acceptable temporary support or go look for someone to serve as a willing assistant. Both of these remedies take you away from the task at hand.

TIP: Here's an inexpensive solution: modify and install a readily available shelf bracket on your workbench. First, screw a 1½–2' length of vertical shelf standard to one leg of your workbench as shown *below*. Then, grab a metal shelf bracket and for the protection of your workpieces face it with a grooved piece of wood or foam, glued in place with epoxy. You may wish to make several brackets of different sizes and configurations to handle special situations. Adjust the bracket up and down for various stock widths. This setup gives you a sturdy, economical, and time-saving support system.

—Tom E. Moore, Madison, Va.

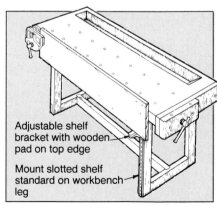

Adjustable shelf bracket with wooden pad on top edge

Mount slotted shelf standard on workbench leg

Workbench Improvements

Handscrews make the best of "edgy" work situations

Although a woodworking vise will hold small pieces of stock on edge, some unwieldy jobs such as planing an edge or drilling holes into the face of an edge dwarf a vise.

TIP: Use a pair of large handscrews to hold each end of a workpiece in place on top of your bench as shown *below*. Start by securing one clamp to the bench. Then, follow these two steps for tightening the clamp holding the workpiece: First, adjust the screw nearest the stock to the thickness of the board. Second, with the clamp jaws parallel, tighten the other screw to secure the board.

—From the *WOOD* magazine shop

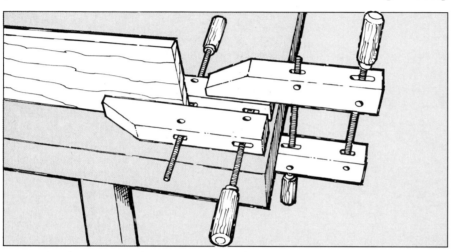

Out on the cutting edge

While at your workbench, have you ever needed to cut a piece of string, cord, or tape—and didn't have a knife or pair of scissors?

TIP: Add an integral string and tape cutter to your bench: To one edge of the benchtop, glue or tack the serrated metal strip cut from an empty box of aluminum foil or plastic wrap. Position it with the serrated edge level with the bench surface, as shown, in a location where you won't accidentally bump into it.

—Wally King, Oakland

A bench hold-down anyone can afford

European-made woodworking benches typically include metal bench dogs and other devices for securing workpieces in place for sanding, carving, and other operations. There's no question they're desirable, but their cost puts such niceties out of reach for many of us.

TIP: Tailor-make hold-downs for your bench by calling one or more of your ¾" pipe clamps into double duty. At suitable intervals (we spaced ours 1' apart in two rows 1' apart along the front of a bench), bore 1⅛" holes through the surface of your bench. Then, screw pipe flanges and wooden doughnuts in place underneath as shown *below*. Thread a length of pipe into the flange, add the clamp, and you have an inexpensive hold-down. To accommodate a variety of stock thicknesses, buy varying lengths of pipe.

—Tom Koenig, Easton, Mo.

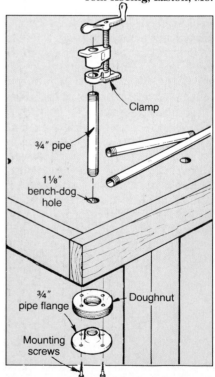

Clamp

¾" pipe

1⅛" bench-dog hole

¾" pipe flange

Doughnut

Mounting screws

Work Supports

Harness a sawhorse to hold your workpieces

Every once in a while, it's necessary to rip, crosscut, drill, or shape workpieces that are just too long to rest securely on the table of a stationary power tool. If someone is available, you could enlist them to hold up the far end of a long piece, but that may actually be dangerous in terms of binding or kickback, depending on the machine and situation. Here's how to assemble some inexpensive supports.

TIP: Use some clamps, a piece of ¾" plywood, and a sawhorse to put together a reliable support for that stretched-out job. The configuration shown *above* works nicely to support long pieces. The second setup shown at *right* proves handy for holding sheet stock as you plane an edge or for securing a door while you install hinges.

—From the *WOOD* magazine shop

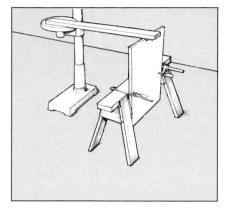

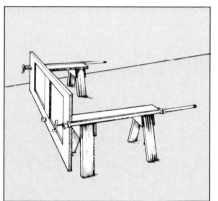

Blocks suited to a "T"

It's tricky jigsaw work to cut along curvy lines on a large panel. The problem: How to properly support the workpiece and provide blade clearance.

TIP: Nail or screw together some T-blocks from 2×4" pieces as illustrated *below*. Four or more of these provide plenty of clearance for any jigsaw blade and support the panel.

—Ralph R. Parschen, Pine Bluff, Ark.

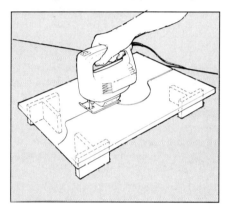

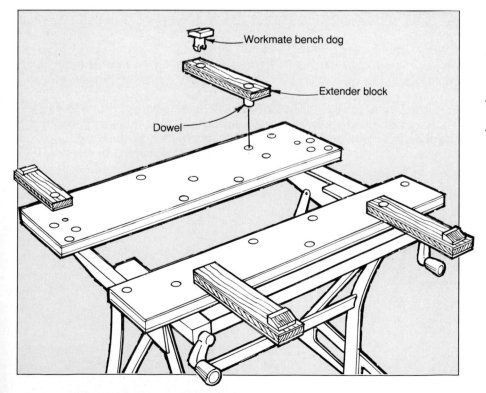

Workmate bench dog

Extender block

Dowel

Workmate extenders increase holding capacity

A Black & Decker Workmate makes a great shop helper, but how often have you wished its jaws would stretch a little further to hold that wide workpiece for sanding, drilling, or routing?

TIP: If you'd like to increase the holding capacity of your Workmate, just add extender blocks to the work surface. From ¾" plywood, cut four 1¾×8" pieces. Bore ¾" holes in both ends of each piece and glue a 1¼" length of ¾" dowel in one end, as shown at *left*. Insert Workmate dogs in the remaining holes. Now, your Workmate will hold a workpiece as wide as 23". You can make the extenders even longer for added working capacity.

—Robert K. Graul, Alton, Ill.

Work Supports

How to improve your adjustable work support

Surely one of the handiest helpers in a shop is the adjustable work support. But, they do have their faults. Light ones, for example, tip easily. And, you often have to try two or three times before you get the height adjustment correct.

TIP: Stabilize those lightweight work supports by adding ballast in a 2-gallon ice cream container or small paint bucket filled with concrete. Lowering the center shaft into a short length of PVC pipe set in the middle keeps the weight in place on its plywood platform (see drawing *below*). To quickly adjust the height for specific tools, score lines on the center shaft and, if you like, make masking-tape labels to remind you what tools go with what lines.

—John Kojeski, Denham Springs, La.

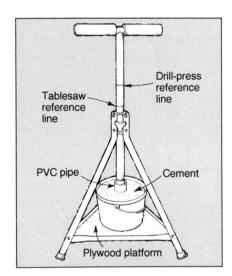

Drill-press reference line

Tablesaw reference line

PVC pipe

Cement

Plywood platform

Temporary protection glide

Wooden legs and supporting panels that rest on the floor—especially plywood ones—may splinter when moved.

TIP: Protect these damage-prone parts by making gliders from smooth hardwood scrap and fastening them to the bottom of the piece with one or two finishing nails, as illustrated *below*. Be sure to countersink the nails at least ⅛″ so that the heads won't mar flooring. When the project is complete, simply remove the protectors.

—From the *WOOD* magazine shop

Bottoms up!

Supporting larger, floppy workpieces while doing inside cutting with a jigsaw can be a challenge. These projects often require a lot of stopping and turning to avoid sawing into the work surface.

TIP: Here's another use for those portable worktables known as Black & Decker Workmates. Turn the table upside down and support the wood with the four legs while using your jigsaw. You'll find this more convenient than sawhorses.

—Dustin Davis, Frostburg, Md.

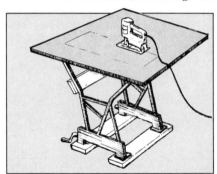

Cushy sawhorses

Because the rough surfaces of most sawhorses can mar a workpiece, you have to work elsewhere when repairing finished furniture.

TIP: Cut 1×4s or ¾×4″ plywood to the length of your sawhorses. Then, cover the strips with scrap carpet and tack the strips to the top beams of the horses with small finishing nails countersunk.

—From the *WOOD* magazine shop

More Terrific Tips

One-string shop apron

Shop aprons always are difficult to tie and untie behind your back, but it becomes a really knotty problem when the strings begin to unravel.

TIP: Snip off both of the old strings and replace one of the strings with a piece of new twill tape (available at fabric stores). Sew one piece of matching nylon hook-and-loop tape to the end of the new apron string. Sew the other half of the fastening tape to the body of the apron. You now can quickly fasten and unfasten the apron with one hand.

—**Myron Nixon, Longmont, Colo.**

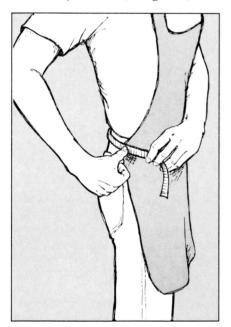

The dry touch

Natural oils in your hands tend to rub off onto unfinished wood. The result is unsightly, telltale flaws that appear only after you apply stain or finish.

TIP: Rub your hands vigorously with sawdust from your shop before you handle the stock. The sawdust will draw out excess oils from your pores and make finishing neater.

—**Larry Bedaw, North Swanzey, N.H.**

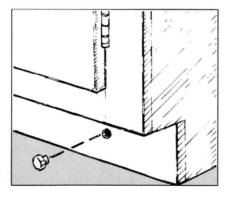

Sawdust

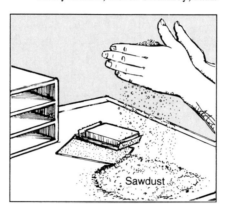

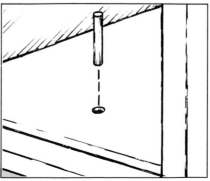

Double-faced tape to the rescue

No matter how hard you try, hinges seem to move slightly when you mark their position.

TIP: Double-faced tape provides an excellent opportunity to accurately position new hinges. Use a sharp knife to mark out the hinge outline and screw holes. Drill the holes and then remove the stock.

—**From the *WOOD* magazine shop**

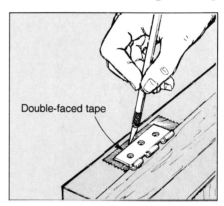

Double-faced tape

Working the bugs out

The space beneath baseboard-type cabinets becomes a popular hiding place for all kinds of household insects. How can you effectively deliver pesticide to the little critters?

TIP: You have two choices:
1 Drill a ⅜″ hole in the baseboard of each cabinet to allow application of your favorite bug killer. Then plug the holes with furniture dowel buttons. Don't glue them in place, so you can pop them out for future raids on the hideouts. Stain the plugs to match the cabinet.
2 Drill a ⅜″ hole through the floor of each cabinet, apply the pesticide, then insert a dowel plug flush with the cabinet floor (dowel must fit snug in hole).

—**James D. Craig, Birmingham, Ala.**

More Terrific Tips

A simply magnetic idea—with a catch

The challenge of installing magnetic catches lies in aligning the strike plate with the magnet.

TIP: First, install the magnet on the cabinet frame. Put the wood screw through the strike plate and place it on the magnet. Close the door and the screw will punch the location hole onto the door. After installation, adjust the hardware as necessary for a precise fit.

—From the *WOOD* magazine shop

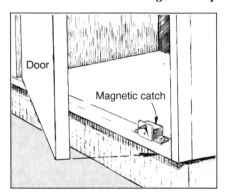

Door

Magnetic catch

Keeping plugged in

How many times have you been left powerless when using a portable sander or jigsaw because the tool cord and the extension cord pulled apart? Now you can stop this frustration with this simple trick.

TIP: Tie a loose overhand knot with the two cords and plug them together. Tension on the knot tightens the union and the power connection stays together throughout your work.

—From the *WOOD* magazine shop

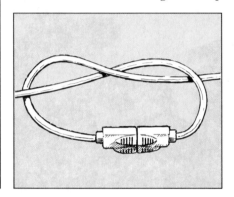

On track for hanging files

Hanging files keep drawers marvelously organized, but they require a metal frame insert to support them. The insert looks out of place in wooden files you've built yourself.

TIP: Mount lengths of ½ × ½" aluminum angle on the top edge of each drawer side, as shown. Now, the drawer will support hanging files so you won't need the standard, unattractive racks.

—Craig K. Carlson-Stevermer,
Arden Hills, Minn.

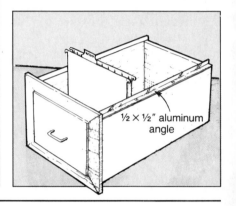

½ × ½" aluminum angle

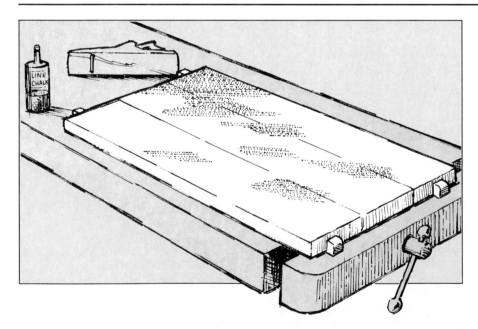

Pinpointing low spots in planed boards

When hand-planing the surface of a glued-up piece you often miss minor high or low spots—even when you use a straight-edge to determine whether the surface is all in the same plane. You may not notice these defects until after staining or other finishing. Then, suddenly, they jump out at you.

TIP: Rub a small amount of colored line chalk on the project surface, then plane it diagonally with very shallow cuts. The chalk stays on the wood depressions as you shave it off, leaving low spots clearly visible. Shading the surface of the wood with a soft lead pencil will do the job, too.

—Robert J. Stehm, Merchantville, N.J.

More Terrific Tips

Bench hook securely holds woodcarving stock

Relief carving requires using both hands on the carving tool. For comfort and safety, securely fastening the carving on a table-top helps greatly.

TIP: You can easily make an inexpensive bench hook to hold carving pieces. Along two adjoining sides of a base of ¾" plywood, attach 1 × 2" rails with 90° notches cut to your needs. Fasten 1 × 2" cleats along two sides of the bottom of the base in the opposite corner from the notches. If possible, hold down the bench hook by securing one of the cleats in a vise. You can omit the bench cleats and clamp the assembly to your benchtop with C-clamps.

—John Roccanova, Riverdale, N.Y.

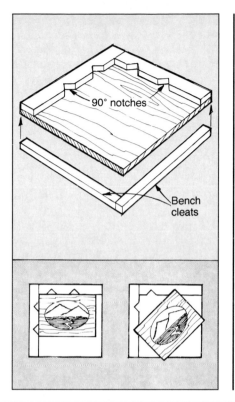

A super solution for misguided scrapers

When scraping wood near the edge of plastic laminates, the scraper accidentally skips across the laminate and does irreparable damage to the new surface.

TIP: Hold a handscrew firmly against the edge trim. Position the scraper in the handscrew as close as possible to the plastic laminate. Tighten the clamp and dress down the surface while the clamp guides the scraper.

—From the *WOOD* magazine shop

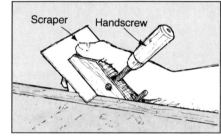

Build self-hanging picture frames

It's great fun to cut your own picture-frame stock and put it together. Unfortunately, conventional hanging devices such as screw eyes with wires or serrated metal hangers don't allow the frame to hang flush against the wall. This is something to consider if an artwork is often viewed from the side.

TIP: As you cut your frame stock, leave an extra quarter-inch of material on the back side for a ⅛" kerf ⅛" deep and ¼" inside the edge as shown at *right*. Hang the picture on two pan-head screws spaced apart on a level line about half the width of the frame. The top of the screw heads should protrude ⅜" from the wall. This way, the picture remains plumb and flush against the wall.

—Keith Hyde, Des Moines

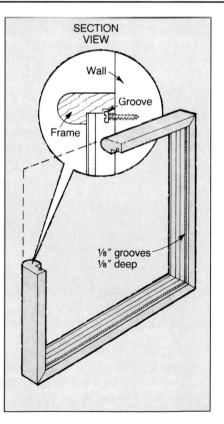

Pushsticks that stick out

Pushsticks have a way of blending in with other scraps of wood around the shop, making them nearly invisible.

TIP: Paint the handles of your pushsticks a bright color (such as red) to make them stand out from the other bits and pieces of wood around the shop. Now you can keep better track of them so they will be handy when needed.

—Terry Leach, Lovington, Ill.

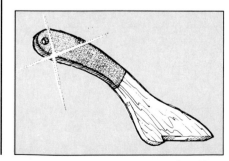

More Terrific Tips

Don't let wood get bent out of shape

Freshly resawed or planed stock will certainly warp when allowed to lie facedown on a flat surface for as short a time as one hour (even faster in dry climates). Moisture will escape from the exposed face of the board at a faster rate than from the side facing down.

TIP: Stand the piece(s) on end so air can flow along all surfaces. Leaving wood this way overnight allows the stock to restabilize.

—From the *WOOD* magazine shop

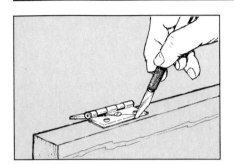

Setting butt hinges

How do you mortise butt hinges so they fit right the first time?

TIP: Start by screwing the hinge in place on the door. Next, use a sharp knife to score the outline of the hinge. Then screw the other half to the hinge of the frame edge, marking and routing or mortising as before. Finally, reinstall the hinge.

Another tip: Because it's so easy to twist heads off brass screws, drill pilot holes and lubricate the screws with wax before installing.

—From the *WOOD* magazine shop

Zap insect invaders

"Surprise" insects in carving blocks and other small pieces of wood can be unpleasant discoveries. How do you get rid of them?

TIP: A quick shot in the kitchen microwave oven will put all intruders out of business. Set the oven on its lowest setting and turn it on for 1 minute. The resulting molecular vibration, not the heat, kills the bugs. To avoid splits, be careful not to overheat the wood.

—John C. Monaghan, Goleta, Calif.

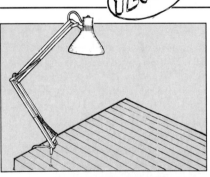

Shed some light on the subject

Overhead lighting often does not offer adequate illumination for doing closeup work. Adjustable reading lamps help, but positioning them where needed can tie up a lot of clamps and your patience!

TIP: It's easy to add an adjustable reading lamp to a work bench. Simply drill holes of the appropriate diameter to accept the shaft that normally goes into a clamp fitting. Drill these holes wherever you need the illumination. Reposition the lamp or remove as needed.

—Carlos Voss, Colton, Calif.

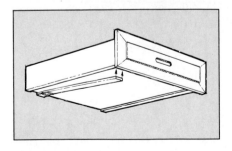

Securing drawers without locks

Young and inquisitive hands have an affinity for exploring drawers in gun cabinets and other off-limits areas.

TIP: Install a 1"-wide blocking stick on the bottom of the drawer so it drops into place behind the frame of the cabinet front. A finger hole bored through the dust panel provides a way to release this latch and open the drawer from below.

—Asa M. Reece, Plantation, Fla.

More Terrific Tips

How to cure your power miter box of splinters

A power miter box is a slick device, but chipping and splintering can be a nuisance.

TIP: Use clamps or screws to secure a ½"-thick birch or maple auxiliary fence. When the slot enlarges after prolonged use, replace it with another auxiliary fence. You'll find these liners particularly helpful when the face side of molding is opposite the cutting direction. Ease your cutting speed to further help with this problem.

—From the *WOOD* magazine shop

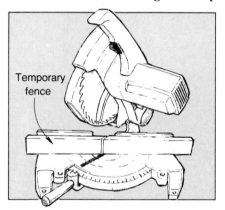
Temporary fence

Avoiding a sticky sticking-door situation

It's not an open-and-shut case to fix a sticking door. Until you find the offending area, you don't know where exactly to attack the problem.

TIP: Place a sheet of carbon paper in the door with the carbon side facing the edge of the door. When you close the door, the paper will leave marks where the bind occurs. You may have to move the paper and close the door several times to get sufficient markings.

—D. Rohoway, Winnipeg, Manitoba

Handy guide for cutting thick, irregular stock

Making accurate perpendicular or angular cuts in thick timbers or odd-shaped posts can be troublesome, particularly when you can't make a complete cut from one side. Often the second cut from the back side doesn't match the first cut, leaving an unsightly mismatch.

TIP: Make a great cutting guide from two pieces of 1×1×14" hardwood and two 10" lengths of ¼" threaded rod fitted with nuts and washers as shown *below*. After measuring the distance between your circular-saw blade and the edge of its base plate, clamp the guide in place. Then, cut one side of the stock to a depth just more than half the stock's thickness, flip it over and cut the opposite side. You can also reposition the guide for angled cuts.

—Tom Xedos, Moreno Valley, Calif.

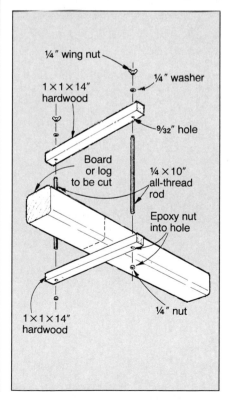
¼" wing nut
1×1×14" hardwood
¼" washer
9/32" hole
Board or log to be cut
¼×10" all-thread rod
Epoxy nut into hole
1×1×14" hardwood
¼" nut

This jig makes for easy scrollsaw blade changes

Because of the small pieces involved, putting a new scrollsaw blade into its mounting clamps can be a hair-raising experience—unless you just happen to have three or four hands. With only two hands, by the time you get everything together, the alignment may be off and the setscrews not tight enough to secure the blade in place.

TIP: Simplify this irksome job by building a jig that holds everything securely in place while you tighten the setscrews. All you need is a pair of small C-clamps, two pieces of scrapwood about 8" long, and a strip of plastic laminate or thin stock to serve as a spacer. You don't necessarily have to epoxy the C-clamps to the block, but doing so will make for quicker and easier changes.

—John A. Henson, Lakeland, Fla.

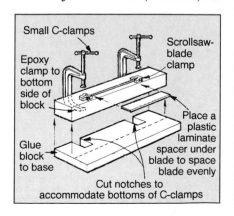
Small C-clamps
Scrollsaw-blade clamp
Epoxy clamp to bottom side of block
Place a plastic laminate spacer under blade to space blade evenly
Glue block to base
Cut notches to accommodate bottoms of C-clamps

Index

Abrasives: powdered, **52. See also** Sanders and sanding
Apron, shop, one-string, **91**
Bandsaws, **2, 61**
Bar and pipe clamps, **5, 7, 9, 20, 58, 81**
Belt sanders, **66, 67, 68, 83**
Bench dogs and hold-downs, **87, 88**
Bench hook, **93**
Bevels, cutting, **74**
Blade-height gauges, **76**
Bolts, cutting, **20**
Bowls, turning, **84, 86**
Bow sander, **64**
Box lids, cutting loose, **72**
Brads, **20, 50, 58, 60, 62**
Brushes: cleaning, **27, 28, 46**; drying, **28**; storing, **19, 26, 27, 28**; uses for, **45, 65**
Cabinets: catches, **92**; hanging, **20**; making, **8, 38**; pesticide use in, **91**
Calipers-setting gauge, **86**
Carving, bench hook for, **93**
Center, finding, **43**; of circle, **40**; of dowel, **42**
Chair repair, **34, 35, 36**
Chisel sharpening, **78, 82**
Chucks **12, 50, 61, 86**
Clamps and clamping, **5-9**; bar and pipe, **5, 7, 9, 20, 58, 81**; edge gluing, **8, 18**; handscrews, **9, 66, 80, 88, 93**; hose, **34**; miniature, **70**; and squeeze-out, **15, 80, 81**; timing, **21**; workbench, **87, 88**
Combination square, **41**
Compass, large-circle, **43**
Contact cement, **19, 22, 23, 29**
Curves: templates for, **44, 56**; trueing, **56**
Cutting guide, **95**
Dado blades, **72, 74**
Dents, removing, **4**
Diameters, measuring, **39**
Disc sanders, **63, 82**
Doors: hinges, **15, 36, 91, 94**; sticking, **95**
Dowels, **34, 38, 42, 75**; kerfing, **37**; storing, **49**
Drawers: rattles, **37**; securing, without locks, **94**
Drill bits: burr removal, **78**; centering, **11, 12**; depth control, **14**; Forstner, **12, 42, 49**; leveling, **13**; modified spade, **12, 13**; small, **14**; straightening, **13**
Drill chucks, **12**; keys, **50, 61**
Drilling debris, **12, 14**
Drilling guides, **11**
Drill presses: chuck key, **50**; for clamping, **7**; for sanding, **67**; stand for, **51**; table

on, **14, 80**
Drills, cordless, **78**
Drum sanders, **65, 67, 68, 78**; dowels as, **64**
Dust control, **10**; lathe, **85**; on safety eyewear, **79, 81**
Edge work, **88**; flush trimming, **55**; gluing, **8, 18**; plywood, **3**; sanding, **66**; trueing, **56**
Epoxy: cooling, **21**; mixing, **17, 25**; on screws, **35**; wiping up, **47**
Equal parts, laying out, **44**
Eraser, pencil, **39**
Face shields, cleaning, **79, 81**
Files, hanging, **92**
Finishes and finishing, **26-33**; applicators, **28, 30, 31**; flaw detection, **29, 32**; furniture, **33**; fuzz removal, **33**; hard-to-reach spots, **30, 31**; mixing, **32**; pinstriping, **29**; protection, **18**; small parts, **30, 32**; smooth, **28, 31**; spray nozzles, **27, 31**; spray touch-ups, **26**; stain, **28, 33**; storage, **27, 30, 32**; stripping, **30, 31, 32**; **See also** Brushes
Flush trimmer, router, **55**
Forming tool, sharpening, **79**
Forstner bits, **12, 42, 49**; substitute for, **13**
Frames: cabinet, **8, 38**; picture, **6, 9, 20, 24, 93**
Furniture: finishing, **33**; repairing, **34-36**; stripping, **30, 32**
Glue and gluing: cap for, **17, 47**; contact cement, **19, 22, 23, 29**; epoxy, **17, 21, 25, 35, 47**; furniture, **34-36**; grain, torn, **18**; laminations, **17, 19, 22**; small places, **15, 17, 23**; smears, detecting, **24**; squeeze-out, **15, 80, 81. See also** Clamps and clamping
Grain: raised, **33**; torn, **18**
Grinders: homemade, **45**; places for, **47, 51**; substitutes, **78, 82**
Grooves, sanding, **68**
Hammers, use of, **16, 20, 22, 24, 79**
Hand protection, **20, 91**
Handsaw blade guard, **62**
Handscrews, **9, 66, 80, 88, 93**
Hardware containers, **48, 49**
Hinges, **15, 36, 91, 94**
Insect control, **91, 94**
Jigsaws, **46, 56, 83, 89, 90**
Jointers, **80**; use of, **18, 70**
Joints, **37-38**; furniture, **35. See also** Clamps and clamping

Knobs, attaching, **25**
Knotholes, patching, **4**
Laminations: bending, **5**; gluing, **17, 19, 22**
Lathe work, **29, 84-86**
Leveling: drill-press table, **80**; hardware for, **36**
Level spot for tools, **51**
Lighting, adjustable, **94**
Magnets, use of, **6, 49, 50, 52, 62**
Masking tape, removing, **29**
Miter box, power, **95**
Miter-cutting safety, **53, 60**
Mitered corners, clamping, **5, 7, 8**; picture frames, **6, 9**
Miter gauges, **72, 73, 76, 77**
Miter stops, **73**
Nails: concealing, **19**; holding, **58, 60, 62**; in picture frames, **20, 24**; removing, **16, 22, 79**; splits from, avoiding, **16, 24**
Noise control, **81**
Nuts: arbor, **74**; wing, **19, 20, 24**
Paint and painting. **See** Finishes and finishing
Paint rollers: drying, **17**; three-inch, **46**
Parallel lines, marking, **39, 41, 42**
Patching wood, **4**
Patterns: rescaling, **44**; templates, **43, 44, 56**; transferring, **39, 40, 41, 42**
Phillips screwdrivers, **83**
Picture frames: clamping, **6, 9**; fasteners, **20, 24**; self-hanging, **93**
Pinstriping, **29**
Pipe and bar clamps, **5, 7, 9, 20, 58, 81**
Planers: storing, **48**; for thin stock, **71**
Planes: blades, sharpening, **78, 82**; use of, **92**
Plugs, **37**; holes for, **12**
Plunge routers, **56**
Plywood: edge treatments, **3**; patching, **4**
Power cords: **10, 60, 62, 68, 92**
Pull string on toys, **61**
Push sticks, **58, 93**
Putty, **3, 4**
Radial-arm saws, **53-54**; for grinding, **82**
Restabilizing wood, **94**
Rip fences, **71, 73, 75, 76**
Routers, **55-57**; bit maintenance, **78, 80, 83**
Safety, **58-62**; drill-press table, **14**; miter cuts, **53, 60**; saw-blade holders, **47, 50**
Sanders and sanding, **63-68**; belt, **66, 67, 68, 83**; blocks, **63, 66, 67**; bow,

64; of bowls, **86**; disc, **63, 76, 82**; in drill press, **38, 67**; drum, **64, 65, 67, 68, 78**; dust control, **10**; flaws, spotting, **29, 66**; pads, **65**; reinforcing paper, **45**; ripping paper, **64**; small pieces, holding, **65, 71**; wheels, **63, 84**
Saw blades: cleaning, **80**; as curved template, **44**; extra life for, **46, 69**; guard, **62**; holders, **47, 50**; honing, **2, 83**; installing, **61, 95**
Sawhorses, use of, **9, 89, 90**
Saws: bandsaws, **2, 61**; jigsaws, **46, 56, 83, 89, 90**; radial-arm, **53-54, 82**; scrollsaws, **69, 70, 95. See also** Tablesaws
Scrapers, **82, 93**
Scratches: detecting, **29**; raising, **4**
Screwdrivers: offset, **23**; Phillips, **83**; protection from, **18, 20**
Screws: broken, **15, 16**; furniture repair, **35**; holes, **23**; lubricating, **21, 24**
Scrollsaws, **69, 70, 95**
Spade bits: level, checking, **13**; modified, **12, 13**
Spindles, sanding, **67**
Stains, use of, **28, 33**
Stops, **53, 54, 55**; miter, **73**
Storage holders, **49, 51, 52**; for saw blades, **47, 50**
Strap clamps, use of, **7, 8**
String and tape cutter, **88**
Stripping, **30, 31, 32**
Switches, safety, **49, 59**
Table inserts, **74, 75, 77**
Tablesaws, **72-77**; blade holders, **47, 50**; safety, **58, 59, 60, 70, 71, 74**; sprucing up, **80**; thin and narrow stock, **70, 71, 75**
Tape: cutter, **88**; dispenser, **52**; double-faced, **2, 8, 16, 19, 32, 91**; masking, removing, **29**
Tape measures, **42, 82**
Tapers, holes for, **12**
Templates, **43, 44, 56**
Thin stock, **69, 70, 71, 75**
Threaded inserts, **25**
Toothpicks, uses for, **23**
Transferring patterns, **39, 40, 41, 42**
Turning, **29, 84-86**
Tweezers, homemade, **22**
Wall paneling, drilling, **12**
Wheels: pinstriping, **29**; sanding, **63, 84**
Wing nuts, **19, 20, 24**
Wood fillers, **3, 4**
WOOD magazine holder, **48**
Work supports, **87, 89-90**